MW00639132

FROM TWO TO ONE

FROM TWO TO ONE

Surviving the Loss
of a Loved One

Rosina Leigh Eller

Dodge
Pond Press

Fernandina Beach, Florida

© Rosina Leigh Eller, 2022

All rights reserved.

No part of this book may be reproduced or transmitted in any form or by any means, electronic or mechanical, including photocopying, recording, or by an information storage and retrieval system, without written permission from the author.

Published by Dodge Pond Press
P.O. Box 200, Fernandina Beach, FL 32035

E-book ISBN 9780976192350
Paperback ISBN 9780976192343

Printed in the United States.

About the cover:

The painting used on the cover is called Don't Rush by the author's late husband, Ron Eller. Two years before he died, he developed a pulmonary embolism, went into a coma, and was on life support for ten days. When he returned home, they knew every moment spent together was a gift not to be squandered. They made a concerted effort to appreciate every moment, knowing their time together was limited.

The importance of this painting and the subsequent series was his realization about appreciating the now. The beautiful and haunting painting is 36" x 48" oil on canvas. It hangs in the author's home where it serves as a loving reminder to appreciate the now and not rush.

Back cover: author photo by Lynne Goodwin

Foreword

By Tim Vandehey

The subject of death and loss evokes endless unanswerable questions. What is the transition point when alive becomes dead—or, as the late Paul Kalanithi put it in the title of his marvelous book, when breath becomes air? Who are we without the people we have built our lives around? What does it mean to grieve? If I don't cancel Amazon Prime, will I be charged for eternity?

Ugh. Too many of those questions lead to epistemological cul-de-sacs and Excedrin headaches, so I'll address two that have long fascinated me and are beautifully represented in this wonderful book. The first is the asymmetry of loss.

Back in 2006, my wife experienced a sudden, terrifying asthma attack that put her on a ventilator for eight days that seemed an eternity. I, a new father of a not-quite-two-year-old daughter, found myself caught in the surreal backdraft: contemplating my young wife's final wishes, trying to decide whether I could remain in the house we'd bought as newlyweds if she died, attempting to keep mind and spirit in one piece through the deep basso thrum of dread that sounded in my ears 24/7. I got a prescription for Xanax and chose not to take it, basked in the love of friends and family, and ended up with PTSD. But that's a different book.

What struck me, even amidst the horrific uncertainty, was the asymmetry of my experience. During those eight days, while I

Dedication

This is for everyone who showed up
when my life was complicated:

- My children for being there when they, too, were experiencing grief.
- My family and friends who listened to my story and didn't attempt to stop my tears.
- My mentors and mentees for their support.
- The widows who came into my life to share their stories of courage and resilience.

And this is especially for my Ron, for always
bringing out the best in me.

Acknowledgments

I want to thank my publisher, Dodge Pond Press, for believing in my book. Writing a book about my grief process was challenging, amazing, and left me feeling vulnerable. But having a publisher who could see the importance of me being true to my experience was amazing. I know you had other projects that you could have chosen, and I remain forever grateful that you chose mine.

Thank you, Nancy Blanton, for beautifully capturing the essence of my book through your outstanding cover design. You incorporate my late husband's art to show a widow who went from being a "Two" to adjusting to being a "One." I love it.

I want to thank Janet Livingston, Lawrence Bienemann, Mary Chapman, and Susan Crossland for their willingness to read through my book. I value and appreciate your various perspectives and feedback. It has made a difference in bringing my work to successful publication.

Thank you, Andrea Patten, for your time and editorial expertise, as I know that this book would not have been possible without it. Documenting my journey through the grief process has been one of the hardest things I have ever done. But sending my very rough first draft to you provided me with possibilities that I had not previously considered. You knew how important completing this book was to me, and I am so happy you showed me that the book is more than grief stories. Thank you for helping me realize that underneath it all, it is a beautiful love story. My love story!

My dream of getting my book published has been a journey. None of this would have been possible without my friend, Trienah Anne Meyers. She introduced me to Amelia Indie Authors, who supported and encouraged me to tell my story. Like millions of others, in 2020 I became very ill and it was not clear that I would survive. One of my regrets was not having finished my book. I shared my concern with Trienah who promised to take my manuscript and get it published. Everyone needs a friend like that.

hovered in the unresolved shadowland between hope and grief, I felt the oppressive weight of death enveloping me like fog. In the ICU, a social worker approached me to discuss my wife's end of life options, only to retreat at the look on my face. I wasn't ready. Is anyone?

Well, yes, but I'll get to that.

Meanwhile, for the people around me, life went on as before, oblivious to my wife's fight for breath. The residents of our charming California surf town went to work, attended school, did laundry, bought arugula at Trader Joe's, and proceeded through the daily clockwork of their worlds, blissfully unconcerned that mine was hanging by a thread. Why weren't they standing vigil as I was, infuriated at the universe's assault on a magnificent woman? How dare their lives go on as though nothing out of the ordinary was happening?

Some of the unreality of loss comes from this appalling asymmetry. Your world has just shattered (or in my case, it appeared poised to shatter every time the phone rang) and yet for everyone else, it's just a Thursday. The kids need to be picked up from soccer practice, and later that night, the game is on.

"Unacceptable!" you want to shout to the heavens. "Everyone should be draped in mourning black and keen like Irish washerwomen! The stars themselves should hide their faces!" For you, life has become an opera of soaring passion and excruciating pain. You're a raw nerve. Why doesn't everyone understand that the world just changed forever? Why hasn't it changed…for them? It feels inexplicable—disrespectful, even, to your loved one.

For the record, my wife recovered. It turned out that her respiratory distress had been due to an allergy even she didn't know she had. She suffered no lasting damage and is fit as a fiddle today. But at the time, that didn't matter. Asymmetry doesn't require death. Hell, it happens after bad breakups, when we're ripped squalling and wounded from a lover's embrace, blinking stupidly, wondering what the hell happened? Loss is loss, and it's an outrage that the world doesn't share our confusion, our desperation, and our constant stumbling to adjust our words and thoughts to the shocking new reality—switching from the present to the past tense, for example.

In From Two to One, the author conveys the feeling of this private purgatory with deftness and grace. Her experience with her husband's slow decline and the inevitability of his end is visible to everyone, but shared by no one. That's the terrible power of loss: it isolates us. That's why, even if you're uncomfortable with grief, even if you don't know what to say, say something. Your gesture of kindness and human-ness might be the touch that helps a grieving person begin clawing their way back to the light.

The other aspect of loss worth unpacking is precognition—rather, how grateful we should be that we don't have it. I should state that for years, I've studied research into consciousness and the mind, and even participated in a study or two, and there is strong scientific evidence that some people do possess precognitive abilities, the ability to accurately perceive future events. But that's not what I'm talking about here.

Early in this book, the author writes that she had no idea that the early symptoms of her husband's illness were a harbinger of what was to come. Isn't that a blessing? Imagine if we could receive accurate premonitions of future events in our lives, like characters in a bad TV series. How would we possibly sleep at night or have peace of mind knowing when our loved ones would be diagnosed with cancer or attempt suicide, or when we would have our last day?

It's far better not to know. That blissful ignorance allows us to live in the moment and experience the joy it contains. It's only in retrospect, in the wake of loss, that we say bitterly to ourselves, "If only I'd known…" No. Remaining oblivious to the future, while receiving the occasional memento mori to remind us of the brevity and preciousness of life and love, is definitely the better option.

Again, I can speak from experience. In the summer of 2021, my family—wife, daughters, parents, sister, future brother-in-law, nephew, nephew's partner—convened in California for a long-awaited reunion after the long sequestration of COVID-19. We spent more than two weeks playing games, making meals, hurling the kind of playful insults that only family can hurl—being together. It was wondrous, and as part of the festivities, we booked a photographer to come to my parents' home and shoot portraits of our family in every possible combination. In the gorgeous summer twilight, backed by a green golf course and hazy blue mountains, we captured the joy of togetherness and made plans for Christmas.

None of us knew that three months later, my mother would be dead. In September of 2021, she had emergency abdominal surgery and developed severe pneumonia. Judy Vandehey, 80, passed away on October 18, leaving my disabled father, who had been with her for literally his entire adult life, heartbroken. Had we been precognitive on those sun-soaked summer days, had we known what was to come, foreboding and terror would have consumed us the way it consumed me when my wife was lying in an ICU bed.

With foreknowledge, it might have been easier to prepare for my mother's passing, but that knowledge would have splintered the delight we took in our carefree, silly, loving time together as a family. And in any case, we handled things quite well.

Earlier, I mentioned that some people actually are ready to have end-of-life discussions about the people they love the most. One of those people was my father. Despite my mother being his whole world, despite his being dependent on her for care, he did not collapse under the weight of his grief. Instead, when it became clear that she would never recover, he surprised us all by stepping up and making the call to change her care order to Do Not Resuscitate, an act of grace and love for the love of his life…and an act of extraordinary courage. I was, and remain, deeply proud of my dad.

So paranormal knowledge of a future loss isn't necessary for us to respond to it with poise, compassion, and bravery. We do that on our own. In fact, the only way seeing the future might prove beneficial would be as a reminder of our mortality, an aide-mémoire that we should savor time and experiences and people while we can. All of us live heedlessly and wastefully on occasion, feeling in the present like the inevitable will never come—like we, out of all the people who have ever lived, will be spared. That's silly, of course; we won't be. But it's precisely our experience of loss that also conveys what a precious thing it is to be alive.

Death and loss don't imply a meaningless universe, nor do they suggest that love is without meaning. On the contrary, the things we care about most are more meaningful because they are finite. Great books, plays, films, symphonies, love affairs…they are consequential, beloved, and beautiful because we know they will come to an end. That is our sorrowful, exquisite contradiction. We're capable of contemplating and craving forever, but it's loss—and the knowledge that we will lose—that shapes us, drives us, and makes us who we are.

That reality, both curse and blessing, is the beating heart of From Two to One. Enjoy.

Tim Vandehey
Kansas City, Missouri

1

Me. Before Him.

After 35, I felt like I'd been in these relationships;
some were great, some weren't so great, but they
weren't right partnerships."
~ Essence Atkins

When I think back at my decisions before meeting the love of my life, I feel blessed for the opportunities that opened the doors needed to get me here. However, as I write about our love and my loss, it is important to share how I got to be me before telling you how we became us.

At thirty-two, I had lived a lifetime; to say that I had been a little lost is an understatement. Even then, some of my choices left me surprised, dismayed, and ashamed. As I matured, life presented me with opportunities for positive change. One such opportunity was meeting the woman who would become my spiritual mentor. Before that time, I didn't believe that I needed guidance, motivation, or emotional support, but as she selflessly shared her experiences and strength, she set the stage for my growth.

Over the years we had multiple conversations about my fear of romantic relationships. We talked about my willingness to settle, not believing that I deserved "more" in an intimate relationship.

1

Eventually, my mentor asked me to list everything I was looking for in a partner. I made a long and comprehensive list, adding as many attributes as I could imagine. A week later, we got together and discussed the thirty-six characteristics on my list. Thirty-six.

The next assignment was narrowing the list to only non-negotiable items. Again we met, and now as I shared my list, my mentor was surprised at how short it was. So was I. There were seven non-negotiable attributes: love, respect, honesty, fidelity, integrity, open communication, love, and acceptance of my son. Any more than these seven attributes, that would be a bonus.

When I dated, I started to look more deeply into the qualities that these individuals embraced. I became willing to do the work it takes to build a healthy relationship. One day I was invited to a party where I noticed a man standing at the edge of the pool. I took a second look and never looked back.

2

The Second Look

"Attraction is beyond our will or ideas sometimes."
~ Juliette Binoche

What is it that attracts one person to another? What was it about this man that made me take a second look? This second look set the wheels in motion for what was to become the next twenty-one years of our lives.

I had been invited to a potluck at a friend's house. I went in, greeted and hugged everyone I knew. When I ventured into the back yard, I saw him for the first time. Standing at the edge of the pool, he was deep in conversation with one of his friends. He was tall, rock-star skinny, with beautiful blue eyes and a great smile. I felt apprehensive as we approached each other for that first conversation. I remember little of what we spoke about, but it was enough to fill my stomach with butterflies and the wish that he would ask for my telephone number.

As we spoke, I was filled with the excitement that only a potential new relationship can bring. This guy expressed himself confidently and gave me his undivided attention when I spoke. As with any possible new relationship, we started by sharing a few of the more interesting stories about ourselves. You know – the ones that make us look good. We spoke briefly of the challenges we faced with our children and our wishes and wants for them. He shared a bit of his work and his passion for art, and I jumped right in to share my love of art, especially of the impressionists. As a result, he asked for my phone number and the possibility of getting together to see a post-impressionist exhibit at the museum. We spoke a bit longer before walking away to mingle with other guests. As the evening ended, I headed home full of excitement and anticipation of our next meeting.

In hindsight, I think about this second look. How the brightness of a future filled with excitement, promise, and hope faded into the reality of his illness, hospitalizations and eventual death. Today, although sad that he is gone, I believe he would be happy and proud that our shared experiences have made me the woman I am today. Equally important is that the love we shared continues to fill my spirit and fuel my writing.

3

The Perspective

*"The family you come from isn't as important as
the family you're going to have."*
~ Ring Lardner

After seven months of dating and getting to know each other, we found ourselves talking about what was in the cards for us. In a restaurant eating breakfast, he said something about moving in together and building a future. As I write this, I realize it may not have been what was said, but the way he said it that caught my ear.

"Wait…what are you saying?"

This time he took a more direct approach and asked me to marry him. I was reminded of the relationship lists I had made under the compassionate eye of my spiritual mentor. I needed to make sure that he understood that my son and I were a package deal. He reassured me, leaving nothing to say but "yes."

I was very much in love, but that was not the only reason I said yes. I was thirty-eight years of age and always ran from this sort of commitment. Marriage had never been a consideration. But I had reached a place in my life where I wanted more. I realized that I deserved more and started to trust that this was a man with whom I could take a risk.

Middle-aged and never before married gave me an unusual perspective – one born of maturity on one hand and innocence on the other. I am very aware of how naive I was and how my inexperience with a committed relationship clouded my expectations. Maturity helped me look for the things we had in common such as the love of our children, the importance of our careers, and the kind of life we could build together. Our values and spiritual beliefs seemed to fit well together, he made an effort to get to know my family, and he was a hard worker. We committed to giving it our all and striving for a marriage based on love, trust, and respect.

The reality is that life happens, and we grow, change and settle into the human beings we were destined to be. Who we were at the beginning is not who we ended up being. I thought I was prepared for marriage, but in reality no one could have been prepared for the future we faced.

However, our love for each other was a constant. Through the years, it grew to include respect, trust, kindness, honesty, and the ability to be vulnerable with each other. Life wasn't easy, but it continued, and we were lucky to love each other until death parted us.

4

The Letter

"I just wasn't one of those girls who dreamt of her wedding day and the birth of her first child."
~ Sarah Jessica Parker

It was time to share our plans with our families. We agreed that the two most important groups were our children and my parents.

The first one we told was my eleven-year-old son, who was delighted with the news and having a father for the first time in his life. Next we phoned his children, aged twenty-four and seventeen, to tell them we were getting married and were planning a trip to San Francisco so everyone could have an opportunity to get to know each other.

My parents were next in line. Given that they lived out of the country, we wanted to make sure they felt included and a part of our plans. Being from a different culture, having a daughter who had given birth to a child out of wedlock and who had indicated early in life that she would never marry… this would come as both a shock and a pleasant surprise. So, we developed a simple plan. As a sign of respect, my fiancè would write a letter introducing himself, and then we would arrange a telephone call to get to know each other.

He wrote a letter to my father saying he wanted his blessing to marry me. Understanding that they had never met, he reassured him that he loved my son and me. He emphasized that he took this responsibility seriously and ended the letter by thanking them for his future wife and child. The letter was mailed, and two weeks later, we all got on the telephone.

When I think back on the conversation I remember how eloquent my father was. He stated that as a grown woman we didn't need his permission but quickly added how much he appreciated the letter and what my fiancé had written. My parents gave us their blessings and seemed at peace that I had a partner and was alone no longer.

Looking back on this event, I am filled with sadness and melancholy, knowing that my parents, husband, and stepson have all passed. However, I also remember the sense of anticipation, excitement, and hope for what our beginning represented – a new family.

5

The Foundation

"You don't marry one person; you marry three: the person you think they are, the person they are, and the person they are going to become as the result of being."
~ Richard J. Needham

I remember the sense of anticipation, excitement, and hope for what our beginning represented – a new family. Coming into this relationship as a middle-aged woman, I was apprehensive; I had a rocky relationship history that included some bad choices. Trusting myself in this area did not feel comfortable. Despite my harsh self-judgment, those experiences gave me an idea of what I didn't want. So, thinking about making a lifelong commitment, drove me to look a little deeper.

My journey began when I started questioning what I wanted out of life. I wanted to be a better mother, friend, and most importantly, a better human being. Before meeting my love, I worked hard to find a "me" I could be proud of. Doors began to open and, with the guidance of my mentor, I learned to focus on the values that I thought would make my life meaningful.

To create a successful partnership, I knew I needed to look beyond the superficial "knowing" I'd settled for in the past. This time I needed to look closely at our values. Which did we have incommon? Were any of the important ones missing? Or in conflict?

We had many late-night conversations; we talked about what we wanted from our lives and for our future. We shared as much of ourselves as possible. As time passed, we continued to share our innermost thoughts, which brought both of us connection and comfort.

In addition, there was an old saying that had become part of my internal guidance. "Actions speak louder than words." The way he treated the "package deal" let me know that we could count on him, that he would be there for us. It seemed that he considered us more of a treasure than a package. I saw the values I was looking for in action. This man showed us love, was honest with his feelings, respected my opinions, and welcomed a ready-made family. This helped me know that we would nurture and sustain a healthy relationship.

I never expected that things would change. We still had our fundamental values in common, but life got very hard. The two people who emerged from those hard things were not the same starry-eyed lovebirds who entered the relationship. I would like to share that we were a bright, shining light through the difficult times, but sometimes faltered. Through illness and hardship, we discovered what commitment truly means. We were steadfast, resilient, and compassionate. We became the people we were going to be.

6

The Shared House

"Home is any four walls that enclose the right person."
~ Helen Rowland

Looking at possible wedding dates, some practicalities within our situation quickly became apparent. My apartment lease would be up in January and his in September, so we decided to move in together with the understanding that we would marry near the beginning of the year.

Through the years I was single, I never "played house." My fear of commitment meant the thought of moving in with someone was not something I considered. Besides, if I ever fell in love the other person would have to understand that I was part of a package deal. As a single mother, I could consider marriage but would not live with someone until then. But now ? I was in love and ready to change many things in my life.

We decided to merge our families early and set up our joint household. We found a lovely three-bedroom townhouse and established a new home for his daughter, my son, and the two of us. Overnight I went from being a single mother with one son to sharing a house with a future husband and stepdaughter. My days were filled with work, and coming home to the demands of a family.

11

I kept the household running, making sure that everyone was comfortable, fed, and their needs were being met. I cooked, cleaned, did laundry, and one day realized that I was overwhelmed. And angry that no one was helping. I went from thinking that I was supposed to be this 1950's housewife who cooked while wearing heels and pearls to feeling like a complete failure in less than a month. There was nothing to do but reach out to my future husband – I just wasn't sure how to do that.

I waited with knots in my stomach trying to figure out how to bring up the conversation. When my partner got home, the look on my face told him something was amiss. He asked, and I told him that I felt like I was failing as a wife, stepmom, and mother. I shared that all this cooking, cleaning, and laundry was much more than I had imagined it would be. He quickly stopped me and said, "we never discussed any of this, and it isn't what we expect of you."

He explained his point of view: this is a family, and families shared – including housework. As he said these words, I could feel the tension melt away, and a moment of clarity hit me. I was the only one with this oppressive vision of what a wife was. Those deeply ingrained superwoman expectations were all mine. Aha! I now understood another big piece of why I had never wanted to marry. My routine changed, some of the work was shared, and we began to settle into the family we were to become.

7

The Scent

"I love paint. I like watercolours. I like acrylic paint...a little bit. I like house paint. I like oil-based paint, and I love oil paint. I love the smell of turpentine and I like that world of oil paint very, very, very much."
~ David Lynch

When my husband and I began dating, he showed me his pen and ink drawings, paintings, completed past projects, and his work as a graphic artist. Anyone who knew him could see how talented he was. I felt blessed to be around someone who wanted – and needed – to express himself through art.

The largest wall in our small apartment was in the kitchen, and it quickly became my loved one's easel. At that time, he worked only with oil paint. I found its pungent smell strong and the ventilation inadequate. When I suggested that he consider changing to acrylic-based paint, he declined. He said that although oils took forever to dry, the depth and the ability to build layers of paint allowed for unique textures on the canvas. Hearing this answer, I knew it was a losing argument, so acceptance seemed to be the key to our future happiness.

As the years passed, that smell I had disliked changed to what

13

I now consider a scent. It became something that I grew to love because it conjured up an image of a happy and productive artist at his easel with his newest creation. Today I am reminded that I miss being immersed in the arts. Even though I'm not an artist, 'art' was something we both appreciated, valued, and had in common.

Somehow this part of me that had brought so much joy to my life seems to have died when he did. Thinking back to a time before our life together, I remembered trips to galleries and museums. I needed to recommit to embracing and nurturing this part of my life. I will make plans to visit some museums and local galleries to see what new artwork has been created. It is time to move forward in search of new scents, textures, and images to feed my heart.

8

The Wedding

*"For me, the only thing that mattered was getting married
in the presence of my family and very close friends.
We did not want a big fat wedding."*
~ Ishita Dutta

My fiancé was a graphic designer and had worked on a project
for an organization that sponsored retreats. One of the retreats
would be held in Las Vegas and, because they liked his work, they
provided us with two suites and tickets to attend any of the events.
The retreat was right up our alley with topics on spiritual enrichment, meditation, and speakers who encouraged, motivated, and
inspired. Looking at our calendars, we decided to attend the retreat
– and to marry that weekend.

Having picked a date, we began planning our wedding and
inviting our dear ones to share the moment. Being older, we did
not feel that a huge wedding was appropriate. Given the fact that
we wouldn't be home near family and friends, we opted instead for
a small intimate wedding to be followed by a reception at home a
week later. Still, getting married in Las Vegas…I'd seen and heard
plenty of stories about the flamboyance I didn't want. I found the
Little Church of the West, listed on the National Register of His-

toric Places. It fit our requirements: small and intimate, subdued, and surrounded by beautiful hardwood trees.

Still, when our wedding weekend arrived, a flurry of activities had to take place. Going to the courthouse to obtain our marriage license was one of them. We filled out the necessary paperwork, and when we got to the line that said "witness," my stepdaughter who had just turned eighteen was able to sign for us. Any time I look at the marriage certificate, I see her name and am reminded of this happy moment.

Everyone coming in from out-of-town arrived a few days early: this was the first time both families would meet. It was wonderful to spend time together, share some meals and just get to know each other.

When Sunday arrived, I was filled with anxiety. The only moments of relief came from knowing that we were all together. We were both nervous. I had avoided this for such a long time and was facing the unknown. On the other hand, he had married before and was rattled about things he knew could happen.

I stood at the back of the church, preparing for the walk down the aisle. My father said that he never thought we would be doing this. I smiled as I thought back on my past pronouncements about never doing this, yet here we were.

Our hands shook as we exchanged vows. I dared to imagine that we could have a life where love was abundant, and we would give this marriage our all. I am profoundly grateful that we merged our families and formed something new and loving. Despite the twenty years of difficulty waiting around the corner, we had a marriage that would last.

9

The Illness

"I choose to live in the present because when you suffer from chronic illness, you don't have a choice. It's day by day, one foot in front of the other. When there is a good day, you soak up that moment. Those 'good selfie' moments are captured because they're a gift."
~ Yolanda Hadid

As a newlywed, I expected some sort of honeymoon period. I envisioned a time when everything would go smoothly: our children would get along, our jobs would remain stable, and everyone would be happy. But that wasn't our destiny.

So much for expectations.

We began to find our way, both in our relationship and as parents in a newly-blended family. Then, one month into our marriage, life happened to us in a big way. My bright, handsome twenty-four-year-old stepson had a schizophrenic break. Overnight he went from working on his master's degree to his own personal nightmare. Also overnight, our family life went from honeymoon to hell.

My husband tried to intervene, working for months to get his son into a hospital setting. The pain on his face was heartbreaking,

17

but worse was trying to support someone who desperately needed it but couldn't accept it. Immediately after the incident, all of his emotional walls went up.

When he eventually found the appropriate placement, I saw my partner's pain as the reality of his son's future became more apparent. The promise of a successful young man with his master's degree faded into a frightening unknown future where illness and uncertainty would forever be present. It was heartbreaking to see their dreams melt away.

After a few months life began to calm down, but the peace was short-lived and perhaps too late. The stress of the initial crisis continued to take a toll and, after only four months of marriage, my husband suffered a cardiac event. I think back to this time and I am reminded how, despite the illness, there was hope that he would recover and we would move on to our happy future.

But then came the next event, the next hospitalization, and the next hospitalization, and the one that followed that one until our family life seemed both unrecognizable and almost unbearable. In a matter of six months, we went through five hospitalizations.

Today I am grateful that we didn't know we were experiencing a preview of the next twenty years of our lives: I don't know that I would have stayed.

10

The Season Tickets

*"The energy of live theater is indescribable. You are just
in the moment for an hour and a half."*
~ Adrianne Palicki

Knowing that my loved one's health was failing, I attempted to provide him with small future events to anticipate. For the last shared Christmas, I set out to find a special gift – an experience we could enjoy together. After a bit of research, I bought season tickets to the theater. It was a gift of six plays and, of course, in my mind, accompanying romantic dinners.

As the season approached, his health continued declining, and on the night of the first play, we got dressed up and went hoping that we would be able to enjoy the special evening. We tried to focus on our night out, but everything about it magnified the impact of his illness. He had difficulty walking to the theater entrance, and once there, it was hard for him to stand while we waited to enter.

The seats I had gotten were in the front row, which while providing a fantastic unobstructed view of the stage, was far for him to walk. Once the play started, he needed to go to the restroom and got up a few minutes before intermission. When he didn't return to our seats, I went to the lobby, and found him on a bench. He had passed out, and with assistance from the staff, was able to find a place to sit. We left the theater and went home. Little did I know that within thirty-two days, he would be gone.

The next performance scheduled turned out to be a couple of weeks after he passed, far too soon for me to return to the theater. All I could think about was how awful the last time had been and how exhausted I felt after our evening out. I did not want to throw the tickets away, so I spoke to a couple of friends and gave them our tickets.

The weekend after the performance, my friends called to thank me for the great seats, to tell me how excellent the play was, and how much they enjoyed being there. Somehow, knowing that someone else could enjoy the production made me feel a little better. Our season tickets gave me some hope that perhaps my future could include a return to the theater.

11

The Gesture

"We need 4 hugs a day for survival. We need 8 hugs a day for maintenance. We need 12 hugs a day for growth."
~ Virginia Satir

When my loved one and I met, neither of us had successfully sustained a long-lasting romantic relationship. I ignored the fact that he had been married a couple of times, and he ignored the reality that I had avoided any real commitment. I had, however, witnessed my parents' union and learned from them that establishing a long, loving, and successful marriage was possible. So I focused on the fact that my husband and I believed that we had been given the tools to create a joyful family.

In the earliest phase of our relationship, we found many shared core values and deep wishes for a successful partnership. Having married and merged our families, we were trying to find a way to develop the closeness we wanted everyone to feel. Even though we were an instant family, I tried to find some kind of gesture to let our children know that they were important, loved, and cared for.

I began to think about who made me feel important and loved. In an instant, a close friend came to mind. Whenever we visited her home, we were greeted with a smile and the acceptance you feel only with immediate family. We always felt loved, and the hugs upon entering her home solidified that feeling. We knew we were wanted and welcome.

Because of this experience, I insisted that we hug our children often and, more importantly, that we expand that concept into a family hug. When someone would call for a family hug, we'd circle up, and for just a short while we would embrace the whole. We were establishing our own traditions, and this became one of my favorites.

The kids thought they were silly, but it's funny how something that started out so contrived ended up becoming something very special. No matter what was going on in our lives, the family hug provided the warmth often missing from a newly formed family. I am so grateful that our family hugs lasted for the remainder of my husband's life and have continued into my new one.

12

The Being of Service

"Service which is rendered without joy helps neither the servant nor the served. But all other pleasures and possessions pale into nothingness before service which is rendered in a spirit of joy".
~ Mahatma Gandhi

Through my life's s and downs, I have worked hard to establish meaningful relationships within my spiritual community. I've developed friendships based on mutual respect, shared spiritual principles, and, often, deep love. I was taught to give back. I just needed the willingness to take action to benefit someone else – to be of service when it mattered.

I was comfortable showing up for others. But I struggled to allow others to support my husband or me. A friend reminded me that my dear one's isolation was not 'about' me. Instead, it was about someone I loved, unable to participate in life because of his illness. I knew she was right and needed to ask my community of friends for help. I felt as if I was imposing. However, the reality was that my loved one was unable to leave our home, and the isolation he experienced was heartbreaking.

I asked a handful of people to visit, share a meal in our home, and become part of one of the most challenging times in our lives. I wasn't surprised that my close friends were willing to give their time, but I was amazed that many acquaintances were also ready to show up.

I developed a closeness to some people because of their selflessness and willingness to be there for us. I began to notice that after these visits, my loved one was less depressed and more animated. I remain grateful that they showed up without asking for anything in return. They came without expectations. They came through the snow. They came with food, and most importantly, they came to interact with a housebound sick and suffering fellow human.

I am forever grateful for supportive friends who were compassionate enough to visit. They showed up month after month. They showed me how vital being of service really is and how meaningful it is to the one who is suffering. These individuals made a difference when it mattered to my loved one and me. I am beyond grateful and know how blessed I am by the people I have had the privilege to get to know during this soul-crushing journey.

13

The Staircase

"A kiss is a lovely trick designed by nature to stop speech when words become superfluous."
~ Ingrid Bergman

Despite my loved one's bad health and inability to work, after twelve years of marriage we were finally able to purchase a home of our own. We made a list of the must-haves and, after searching for a month, we found our perfect New England home. The three-bedroom modified colonial had an open floor plan and sat in the middle of three and one-half acres.

Each of us had a favorite part of the house. My husband's was the 1100 square foot basement which he quickly converted into his art studio. There were several spots that made this a wonderful home for me: the fireplace, the three-season room, and the staircase.

When we lit the fireplace, it filled the room with a glow that warmed my body and heart. The flames brought a calm that made our living room the place I wanted to be after a hectic day.

Living in a home surrounded by woods made our three-season room a fabulous place to spend time. I tried to sit on the window bench a few times per week. Early in the morning, the light streamed through the trees while I enjoyed the peace and solitude as well as the occasional strolling deer, turkey, or fox.

But my favorite place in the house was the staircase. On those steps, I felt a deep connection to my loved one. Did I mention that he was tall? And I am not?

Those steps helped us share a unique intimacy: I would lead him to the staircase, climb onto the first step, and turn around to face him. Placing my arms around his neck, we kissed.

At five and a half months since my partner passed, each time I made my way to the second floor, I remembered what those steps meant to me. The first step gave me the height that made our kisses feel glorious, wonderful, sensual, and intimate.My grief had threatened to erase the tender moments on the staircase. Despite missing him, I am grateful for the memory.

14

The Home

"Home is the nicest word there is."
~ Laura Ingalls Wilder

Early in our marriage having limited family in the area, my husband and I were blessed to be welcomed into the fold of a group of friends. We were shown real friendship and the blessings that come with sharing our home with others. I have multiple memories of love shared, where laughter was abundant and hours were spent around the kitchen island cooking and talking with our children and our friends. Creating a warm and caring home was our goal throughout the marriage, and it was one of our most significant accomplishments.

Having this kind of ambiance was of utmost importance to us, but as it turned out was important to our friends who had become more like family. And as a family, they showed up when it counted. In an attempt to provide my loved one with a physically safe and emotionally satisfying home, changes had to be made. For safety, physical modifications were made to our home. One priority was to give my husband easy access to the things he needed. One of the most important safety changes was moving his basement studio to our first-floor library. Our friends came over and within a couple of hours had moved and set up this new space allowing him to paint, be creative and do the things he loved.

Once he became homebound, emotional support was more difficult to access; his immune deficiency meant we could only have a handful of people at the house. Invitations were extended to sit around our dining room table eating, playing cards, conversing, and enjoying whatever laughter we could muster. It was an attempt to provide him with a love-filled social life during his last year.

After his death, I didn't want any signs of sickness around. The first things to be removed were the valuable and necessary items that had kept him alive: oxygen, medications, life alerts, bandages, and the like. Then, our friends changed his upstairs studio back into the library it had once been. But a funny thing happened. I tried but failed to erase the bad memories. The worst part was that it no longer felt like the home it had once been. Tangible signs of illness were gone, but my memory had captured all the sights, the smells, and the sounds of that last, terrible year.

In my heart, I knew that things would never be the same. However, I told myself that my home can be different, project the warmth I am craving, and become welcoming again. I need to start inviting people back into my home but, most importantly, into my life. The memories of opening the door, sharing stories, and having a meal with friends give me hope.

15

The Bad Behavior

"Most bad behavior comes from insecurity."
~ Debra Winger

Two months after our wedding, our twenty-four-year-old son had a psychotic and shortly after that my husband's heart problems started. Although I processed each as a singular crisis, believing we would soon get our lives back. However, in our case, we had a crisis, then another, and another, and until the end arrived, twenty years later.

Being in love and newlywed, I tried to manage the health of another human being without a complete picture. There wasn't one. He dealt with uncertainty, fear, and endless testing, which provided minimal answers. Every subsequent health crisis tore at his tolerance and added frustration. Despite trying to keep himself together, the length of the hospital stay or the friendliness of the attendants could set off wild mood swings.

After several years and multiple surgeries, I found myself tolerating unacceptable behaviors. As a caregiver, I was his advocate. I picked up and managed numerous prescriptions, helped with showering, dressing, and the like, cooked and cleaned, adapted the house to accommodate his limited mobility, and was his driver. But my role as his wife was to provide support.

We had three big arguments during our marriage, all of them taking place in a hospital. Life wasn't easy, and one day after an outburst, I reached the end of my tolerance. We had a loud and long-overdue conversation during which I told him that I loved him and would continue to be his advocate, but only if he changed the bad behavior. The conversation ended with a warning that if the behavior continued, I would no longer be there for emotional support, nor would I come to the hospital under any circumstances.

As I think back, I learned that severe illness affects everyone differently. We all have different coping skills, and the unacceptable behavior that crept into our lives didn't show up overnight. It was gradual, and we made excuses. Finally, I had to take responsibility and ask some questions. What would I tolerate? What would I excuse? And finally, what could I forgive but never forget? Eventually, I realized that people treat you as you permit. Everything changed. The boundaries set in that hospital room lasted for the remainder of his life. The lessons I learned have carried through into mine.

16

The Unintended Path

*"For every path you choose, there is another
you must abandon, usually forever."
~ Joan D. Vinge*

I often wonder why my life has played out as it has. What if I hadn't gotten involved with the handsome skinny guy at my friend's potluck? Where would I be at this very moment? Occasionally I question whether taking another path would have spared me the years of illness, pain, fear, and exhaustion. Then the fog lifts and clarity finds me.

I have become the combination of all my experiences. My path included more than pain and loss: some times were full of happiness and love. Had I chosen another direction, I would not have the memories of our wedding that included watching my new husband's eighteen-year-old daughter embrace my twelve-year-old son because they were now related. I would not have been at the hospital to see my first grandchild born because my "stepdaughter" insisted that both of her mothers be present to witness the moment.

Another path and I wouldn't have memories of us driving to another state for a family wedding and staying around to see the

4th of July fireworks in Boston. There would be no mental pictures of my family seated on the floor waiting for their silly Santa-hatted parents to hand out presents on Christmas morning.

This path gave me the experiences necessary to help me grow. It provided me with opportunities to embrace the hope, compassion, and unconditional love I needed to survive the circumstances of our lives. The uncertainty that clouded our future also provided the moments of love-fueled closeness or the intimacy we attained. This path still shows me how blessed we were, and today, I recognize that I am exactly where I am supposed to be.

When I find myself reviewing my original expectations for a storybook ending, I see that there were curves and detours in the path. While they were marked with sadness and uncertainty, the other side of that path was full of unimagined wonders including opportunities for travel, marriages, the births of grandchildren and the fulfillment of creative dreams. The other side of the path was a life beyond our wildest dreams.

As I look at our ending, I am grateful for the courage that allowed me to fall in love and let my beloved have a meaningful place in my life.

By writing about my path and how we became us, I have been able to let some of the pain and grief go. As I share my life experiences with you, I hope that they will provide the hope necessary to help you walk through whatever difficulties are in your path.

17

The Storybook Ending

"When you dream as a little kid, you dream about storybook endings and storybook players and scenarios like that."
~ Gerrit Cole

One of my greatest fears growing up was being in a relationship where I would have no control over living my life. The fear of getting married was so persistent that it prevented me from ever envisioning a storybook ending. However life does go on, and becoming a single parent opened me up to take a good look at my beliefs, my history, and all those stubborn patterns. I began to see other possibilities for my future, trusting that not all relationships would limit me. I fell in love with this man who accepted me for who I was.

We used the traditional vows when we married and added a few personally meaningful thoughts to the ceremony. I realize now that I never really paid attention to the part that said 'for better, for worse, for richer, for poorer, in sickness and in health.' As a newlywed I never anticipated any of the negatives. My inner child's fantasy was that I would fall in love and everyone would be happy. That storybook ending included: happy children, financial stability, everyone in love, and, most importantly, everyone healthy.

The story in my head definitely did not include hospitals, depression, unhappiness, and death but life has a way of happening in its own way. In reality, I had to stretch my underdeveloped parenting skills, become the only breadwinner, navigate the medical system, and provide an almost unimaginable level of emotional support to others. I was not prepared. I'm not sure anyone ever is.

18

The Renewal

"I think it's time to have a celebration of life and renew our vows. And this time we're going to write the vows because they're going to mean a lot more. We certainly put the 'in sickness and in health' vow to the test the last year and a half."
~ Bill Rancic

I woke up on a beautiful warm Sunday to a clear blue sky full of bright, shining sunlight. The day's goal was to organize a couple of photo albums that I had inherited from my mother. The plan was to open up the albums and sort through all the pictures; as I opened the first album and turned the page, however, I found the invitation my loved one created for our small wedding reception.

As I read, the words seem to jump off the page "Rose promised Ron a rose garden" and "Ron promised Rose a colorful life." I remembered the sentiment that went into saying those words and how we wanted our vows – our solemn promise – to represent us. I never gave him a rose garden, but I worked hard to landscape our property with all the perennials I could get my hands on. As for a colorful life, all I have to do is look at any wall in my home to see his vibrant colors and fabulous images documented in oil.

After nineteen years of marriage, we began discussing the idea of renewing our vows for the upcoming twenty-year milestone. We thought of having a small celebration at home with a justice of the peace and a handful of friends. We would write the vows that represented everything we had gone through – the challenging part would be to share what we wanted for the next twenty years. Given the state of his health, we knew this would be a lie, but there was something about just "acting as if" and opening up our hearts to share all the love we felt.

When you live from one crisis to another everything becomes overwhelming. As time passed, it became clear that the progression of my husband's illness continued unabated. As I sorted through the pictures, I'm reminded of how difficult his last year was. He was very ill; we were always tired and overwhelmed. This prevented us from the celebration we imagined, but we could still acknowledge our twentieth by having dinner with close friends. It never occurred to us to bring the justice of the peace to the house and exchange our vows in private.

But today I understand that we didn't need to have a caterer or a party – we reaffirmed our commitment to each other and to the love we shared by the way we lived each day. Looking through the remaining photographs, I am grateful for the invitation my mother saved and the reminder of how lucky we were to have found each other and celebrate twenty years of loving marriage.

19

The Gift of Time

"It's only when we truly know and understand that we have a limited time on earth – and that we have no way of knowing when our time is up, we will then begin to live each day to the fullest as if it was the only one we had."
~ Elisabeth Kubler-Ross

Twenty-six months before my husband's passing, he was admitted to the hospital with a pulmonary embolism and to my horror I watched him get progressively worse. Close to death, they admitted him to the Intensive Care Unit where he received the care required to save his life. After six days in a coma and on life-support he was transferred to a step-down unit. It took a while before he could leave the hospital, but once he came home, the reality of how blessed we were became clear. By all accounts he should have died. We both knew that we had been given the gift of time. There was not a moment from that point forward that could be squandered in conversations not had, hugs not given, and love not shared.

The importance of this gift could not be ignored, and because of it, we made a conscious decision to be as honest with each other as possible. Knowing how close my dear one had come to death somehow opened the doors to conversations we had never had. His life had been extended for an unknown time and this gave us the luxury of speaking about everything and anything. No topic was off-limits, and we hoped that this would minimize any regrets as we approached his end.

The funny thing about knowing that the time we have is a gift is how easily that fact is forgotten. I remember that my sweetheart and I tried to live each day with laughter, determination, purpose, and love, but somehow that reality died with him. It didn't seem to carry over to my widowhood even though I knew better than to waste any of my days.

In a moment of clarity, I recognized the missing piece that had previously enabled me to live each moment of each day as a gift: gratitude. I try to be grateful for this moment, grateful for this day, and, despite my deep grief, grateful for my life.

Today I need to remember the commitment we made to live each day as if it were the last one. Knowing that it can be gone in a blink, I make a personal commitment to not waste the daily gift of time given to me.

20

Another Darned Defining Moment

"A defining moment takes a long time to get over if you ever do."
~ Mick Jones

If we are lucky, life provides us with moments that define our direction, our future, or how we see our reality. Some of these moments are inspiring, while others can be pretty painful. I am fortunate to have experienced some defining moments that changed how I saw and dealt with my loved one.

At one time, the progression of my husband's illness was so gradual that I didn't always notice the subtle deterioration. One of my defining moments occurred at a barbecue. Friends had gathered to play games, eat barbecue, and just enjoy the spectacular weather. But as we entered the yard, I noticed their reactions. It was the first time I realized how much my darling's physical condition had changed. And as we left, a young woman cried as she watched him struggle to reach the car. In that one moment I saw him differently. But I adjusted to the new normal and our life together continued.

Six months later I was on a business trip when he called to tell me he had fallen. He described enormous bruises, I could hear how upset he was, but he assured me that he was fine and we would talk

when I got home. Upon my return, I saw how badly he was bruised
. He told me about losing his balance and feeling unsure of himself. He said that he wanted some kind of medical alert device, and
I quickly let him know that it was unnecessary, that he was only
sixty-four years old, still strong, and would be just fine.

A couple of days later, he got intensely dizzy while walking and
reopened the topic. I was still opposed to getting the device, but
my heart sank when he said that he felt unsafe being in the house
alone. This was my moment – a defining moment – when I realized
how sick he was and that I was the only obstacle that needed to be
dealt with. I made some calls and within twenty-four hours, we had
a medical alert system in place.

At about this same time I was experiencing one of the deepest
feelings of financial insecurity I had ever felt. I prayed and meditated to do everything in my power to simply pay the bills and tried
to resist thoughts about what my financial future would hold.

In the past, my husband had always been able to help me
through feelings like this. Once his illness prevented him from
working, I became the primary breadwinner and for many years
had made all the financial decisions. I had been responsible for
ensuring everything was taken care of, including him. One of the
decisions I made was to obtain a line of credit to remodel a bathroom for accessibility. As the reality of his life ending became a
certainty, I was left with this looming financial exposure and no
clear way to manage with it.

I made a valiant attempt to block these thoughts. But the harder I ignored, the bigger they got. Still, I took some times to create
the perfect script for what needed to be said and how. There was no
escaping the conversation I needed to have with my loved one. And
I didn't want to feel like a ghoul in the process.

But before I could take action my partner approached me, and
I confessed that I was living in fear due to our debt. As we talked,
I realized that I had been afraid to have a conversation about a
future that no longer included him. As we discussed our finances I
became a little less burdened, and we came up with a plan. I could

see the relief on his face knowing I would be taken care of after he was gone.

Together we decided to consolidate our debt and buy a dependable new car ensuring my ability to continue our lives without the financial anxiety I had been living with. The plan we agreed to that long-ago day has made my present life possible.

As I write this, I am still ashamed of being so unaware, and in denial so deep it kept me from seeing how sick he truly was. And also of trying to force him to share my denial by not allowing him to help me while he was still alive. These were defining moments, and helped me reach a deeper level of acceptance. Because of them we were able to ensure our mutual safety.

21

The Multi-Colored Fingerprints

*"You can't change your fingerprints. You have only ten of them.
And you leave them on everything you touch;
they are definitely not a secret."*
~ Al Franken

Meeting and marrying an artist enabled me to recognize how creative souls use their gifts. My loved one was always doing something, and knowing that his time was limited, he refused to waste any of it. He would spend endless hours expressing his innermost thoughts through painting and occasionally by using his computer. It was his way of losing himself into creativity instead of the dread of his illness. However, as his condition progressed the medium for his expressions changed to writing, and using graphic programs on his computer. On occasion he would use a pad and pencil.

In the last year of his life, he wanted to paint, but he felt trapped by his oxygen hose, so our friends converted our small library into his studio. This enabled him the freedom to plan the subsequent few paintings and the flexibility to execute them when he was able.

Every morning as I went off to work, I would glance at his easel to see where he was in the process. Given how quickly he tired and his lack of stamina, I knew how taxing these last paintings would be. However as each day passed, I could see incremental changes to the canvas, and then one day, like magic, it was done. He had cleaned up the paintbrushes and left everything ready for his next painting.

Coming home that day, I stopped to admire the painting as it sat drying on the easel and happened to glance at the doorway when I noticed his multicolored fingerprints on the door jamb. It was still wet and could have easily been wiped away as oil paints dry very slowly, but I left them there.

Little did I know that the completion of this particular piece of art would be the last oil painting he would ever do, and the fingerprints on the door jamb would be the evidence that this is where it was created. I am so grateful that I never wiped the door jamb clean or painted his fingerprints away. It is a reminder that he was here and he was loved. His fingerprints are still tattooed on my heart.

22

The Temporary Gift

"I believe that we are here for each other, not against each other.
Everything comes from an understanding that you are a gift in
my life – whoever you are, whatever our differences."
~ John Denver

After years of being single, I found that special partner. The one you know is the right one because of how easy it is to navigate life when you are together. From that first time I saw him standing by the pool's edge, we started talking and never stopped. This was the gift that I had imagined, prayed for, and finally received.

What I find interesting is that with all the talking we did, I never paid attention to the conversations regarding his health. My partner was upfront, and because I had never loved anyone like this before, I now realize that I heard his words through very naive ears.

As time passed, the reality of his health problems shattered any illusions I might have had, and it became evident that his illness was fatal. Despite the never-ending medical issues, I found that we somehow managed to continue to nurture the love we shared. Caring for this love was complicated and emotionally draining due to our shared truth: we would not be having a happy ending and we both knew it.

I often find myself in my three-season room thinking about the time we shared. Spending those years with my loved one gave me my first real experience of sharing everything with another human being. The intimacy and trust that was forged came with many harsh realities. But accepting and knowing my partner's fears, joys, and aspirations and allowing him to see mine set the stage for something extraordinary. Despite the sadness I feel regarding his death, we had twenty incredible years together. I understand that many people are not afforded that gift and I continue to be grateful that we were.

23

The Unspoken Promise

*"Promise keeping is a powerful means of grace in a time when
people hardly depend on each other to remember
and live by their word."
~ Lewis B. Smedes*

The last few years of my loved one's life included many conversations centered on what was to be done with his artwork and
how long we should keep his website running. Knowing his time
was limited, he made every moment deliberate, and every decision
related to his legacy was intense.

The last time he entered the hospital, all he wanted was his
computer and iPad so he could continue to draw. Working on his
laptop was one of the main ways he dealt with illness-related stress.
When his cardiologist told us that the procedure would take place
the following Monday, my husband spent the entire week working
on this one digital painting.

Every bit of energy was spent completing this last piece of
art. So the day before his surgery, the doctor reminded him that he
would need to let me take his computer home because he needed
to rest as much as possible. At eight p.m., the nurse came in to
remind me that visiting hours were over and they needed to prep

him for surgery. There was no hiding the agitation he felt because he could not print this final painting. This untold story was his last story on canvas: fourteen days later, my beloved husband died.

Months later, I felt terrible that I had not completed this final task. I didn't know how to use the large format printer. We had a close friend who worked with computers, so I mustered enough humility to ask for help. Our friend understood how important this was to me, came to the house, and after a lot of work on the computer and printer, printed this last piece of art. This artwork was my loved one's business, and he trusted I would take care of his legacy.

When I was alone in the house again, I went down to the studio and looked at the print while it lay on the floor to dry. Tears streamed down my face knowing that this was his last piece of art. I appreciated how strange and wonderful it was, and I am forever grateful that our friend helped me fulfill my unspoken promise.

24

Three Times a Robot

"I'm a man on a mission."
~ Kamaru Usman

I hear the word "robot" and I am reminded of the times that others used that word to describe me. I don't believe they intended to be critical or judgmental – it was more of an observation on their part. In hindsight, it was a very accurate one.

The first time I displayed this behavior was when I received a call saying that my mother had an aneurysm burst, was brain dead, and on life support. I immediately went into action and within twelve hours was on a flight to Florida with my son and my husband. I remember my desperation and determination to get there as quickly as possible to see with my own eyes how she was. The feelings of sadness, heartbreak, and loss didn't surface until after the action: they found me in a chair in the intensive care unit twenty-four hours later. I was on auto-pilot from the moment I answered the telephone to the first tear shed in the hospital room.

The second time was after my loved one was hospitalized for a pulmonary embolism. I was at the hospital for two and a half weeks praying, worrying, and sitting by his side while he was on a ventilator. A friend provided support while two of our children flew in to be with their father. When the crisis was over, I had a conversation with my friend as she described how I would rush from one area of the hospital to another, making sure that everything was being done to care for him. Once again I was set to auto-pilot, and remember her telling me to "just breathe."

And now, for the third time in my life, I am walking around robotically, awaiting his last breath. I am numb, mechanical, and functioning only when directly faced with a task. Today I allow myself to be just where I am, anxiously waiting for the next responsibility. I grasp onto the hope that somehow God will give me a few moments of detachment, make me more of a robot, so I can survive these feelings of overwhelming pain.

25

The Psychiatrist

"Your grief path is yours alone, and no one else can walk it, and no one else can understand it."
~ Terri Irwin

In the last week of my husband's life, I reached out to his psychiatrist as end-of-life decisions had to be made. I knew the final decision would not be mine; however, my loved one would be looking for my thoughts. Picking up the phone and explaining our dire circumstances, he immediately scheduled an appointment for the next day.

Arriving at his office early, he took me inside as soon as I arrived. He asked all the appropriate questions, and I shared how I was utterly devastated over the thought that my loved one was going to die. He listened and provided the necessary support, encouraging me to reach out if I needed to talk.

26

The Last Kiss

"A kiss is a secret told to the mouth instead of the ear;
kisses are the messengers of love and tenderness."
~ Ingrid Bergman

I have often thought about the night before my husband died: it was one of the most stunning times of my life. I am often filled with heartbreak and memories of our last kiss or, more precisely, my last kiss.

That Monday, we had spoken with the doctors about no longer extending his life. He had been in the Intensive Care Unit since his open-heart surgery, and virtually every one of his systems was starting to fail. He was suffering unbearable pain and, due to his severely compromised lungs, no pain medications were given. His kidneys were failing so his physicians wouldn't allow him to have any water. The last two weeks of his life in the ICU were incomprehensible, inhumane, and nearly impossible to describe. But there I was, all day and most of each night watching him suffer. I didn't want him to be alone. The worst part was that I couldn't do anything for him. Nothing. Not even give him a glass of water.

According to his last wishes, the defibrillator was turned off, and dialysis was discontinued and he was placed on palliative sedation. We were told that he wouldn't live more than twenty-four hours, so phone calls were placed to inform our family, and friends. We knew it was the end – of his speaking, of his suffering, and of his life.

My denial was still running so deep that I thought about going home to get some rest. But as the afternoon progressed, the nurse set up a comfy chair with a pillow and blanket: she knew that this would be the last night that we would physically be together. I sat in the chair and listened to the murmuring of the hospital monitors and his ever-slowing breath. The reality of this last night was overwhelming. I realized that these last hours were our last hours; they were the countdown to the end of my life with him.

I wanted to keep busy because this kind of pain is unimaginable. But the thought of keeping busy seemed like a betrayal. How do you stay busy as someone you shared life with dies? The answer is you don't. I was alone and didn't know what to do except to stare at him and hold his hand. I prayed for god's grace to take him. I didn't want him to go, but any desire to prolong his suffering was unconscionable.

Through the evening, a handful of friends came to pay their last respects, spending a few short moments before they left me alone with my beloved and my thoughts. I got up to give him what turned out to be our last kiss: it was one-sided and lacked the passion I felt in my heart, but it was full of the kind of love that lived deep inside my soul.

A few more friends came. We shared hugs and tears, and they said their final words to my loved one. In the morning, another came to support me. Numbly, I waited for our children to rush in from the airport and spend final moments with their father. The hours passed too quickly, and at 12:16 p.m., he opened his eyes, took his last breath, and passed away. Even though the end was inevitable, it still hurt to watch these final moments.

When I think back on this day, I am grateful that the end finally brought relief from his suffering. He was surrounded by love. There was a moment of comfort and a belief that he was truly in a better place. I understand that this is an experience not afforded to everyone and know I will be forever grateful to have stayed, to have held his hand and to have sent him off with a loving goodbye kiss.

27

The Guilt

"A voice is a human gift; it should be cherished and used,
to utter fully human speech as possible. Powerlessness
and silence go together."
~ Margaret Atwood

Something was festering in my conscience: I should have said something about my husband's last surgery. The surgery we all knew he had the barest chance to survive. The surgery his doctor said would be his only chance. All I can hear in my head is that I should have said something. If only I had said something, he wouldn't have had that surgery. He would have come back home and been comfortable while we waited for the next heart attack to end his life. He would have been surrounded by people and things that he loved. I should have said something. "I should have." I. Should. Have.

How do I walk away from the regret of "I should have?" I tried praying for the guilt and shame to leave me. But that did not help. I saw a psychiatrist who noted that he was sure my loved one knew that he did not have a chance and that most people in this situation still pick the slimmest of chances of survival over inaction.

I realize the post-surgical nightmare clouds my thinking. Every physical system failed, he made a conscious decision to let go, to allow himself to die. I should have said something.

My guilt and regret are amplified by shame. Shame makes me want to hide the truth. My shameful truth is that I was just tired of it all: the hospitals, the illness, twenty-four-hour caretaking, my fear and hyper-vigilance. I was just plain tired of waiting for the next crisis.

I didn't think it was OK to have these thoughts. EventuallyI discovered that other caretakers had felt the same way. The shared experience reminds me that I am human.

I finally reached out to a trusted friend who recommended that I journal to release some of my pain. I hope that writing will remove some of the power guilt has over me. I believe my loved one made the best decision for his life and trust he would not want me to feel guilt or regret. Remembering this brings some comfort. One lesson learned from this experience is to say what I am thinking to avoid any future 'I should have said something.'

28

The Confession

"The end of confession is to tell the truth to and for oneself."
~ J. M. Coetzee

One morning I found myself remembering a conversation, actually a confession, that had taken place at my kitchen island with two women who I thought were my friends. This confession was an attempt to care for myself by sharing the horrible pain I was going through as I watched him deteriorate into someone I didn't know. It had been a very difficult month, I was exhausted and had reached the point of frustration, fear, and anxiety that only a caregiver of a terminally ill family member can have.

These were my friends, and I believed that whatever I shared would be fine; however, being in this fragile state, I verbalized that I couldn't stand watching him suffer, and I wished that my loved one would die. I immediately noticed the look of horror on my friends' faces, and then I saw how quickly it changed to judgment.

I changed the conversation at that point, but I was left with a pit in my stomach that I feel whenever this memory invades the little peace I have. Apparently, it's one thing to think and quite another to share it. After speaking with them and seeing their reaction I knew that this thought needed to die with me. I realized that this thought should never again be shared, and just having this thought made me feel guilty.

I have since learned that having these thoughts is natural. Being a caregiver to someone ill and suffering is an endless nightmare. It didn't matter what I did, how much I planned because the end result was going to be the same and the best that I could do was recognize that I couldn't control or change how much my loved one was suffering.

I remind myself that despite the thought of wishing that he died, I was a wonderful caregiver. I was there for every hospital stay, physician appointment, and home recovery. I know how draining and depleted your soul can get if you don't emotionally, spiritually, and mentally take care of yourself. Knowing this hasn't changed the remorse over sharing my thoughts with people who didn't understand and who I allowed to shame me. This experience is one that you have to live through to understand the feelings of desperation and pain as you watch someone you love suffer. I don't regret what I thought or felt. I only regret that I used bad judgment in sharing it with these two women.

29

The Letting Go

*"People in grief need someone to walk with them
without judging them."*
~ Gail Sheehy

I was a woman on a mission – I just didn't know what that
mission was. Our children flew in on a Tuesday, and my loved one
died three hours later. Despite knowing there was much to be done,
I was so distraught that I was paralyzed. I reached out to a friend
for help, and she arranged a meeting at a funeral home the next
day. Recognizing my powerlessness, I asked my daughter to take
the reins for planning her father's services, and she immediately
went to task.

Planning a funeral when your family lives on another coast
adds a layer of complexity. To decrease the burden, she began dele-
gating tasks to other family members. Arrangements were made for
my son's wife and in-laws to come in from Seattle and Denver, and
my daughter's husband and my two granddaughters to fly in from
Los Angeles. Everyone was coming to pay their last respects and
support me and each other.

Our house was abuzz with activity as our children searched for
a picture and a painting for the wake and funeral services. Someone

gave me various menus to choose refreshments for the gathering after the services. The search began for passwords as we knew we needed to back up my loved one's computer and all his artwork.

Everyone was busy doing something; I felt distant from everyone and everything around me. I knew I was physically and emotionally exhausted after the previous three weeks but sitting and just waiting for family to arrive seemed surreal. I sat at home as a steady stream of friends gathered. Some brought flowers, others brought food, but the bottom line was that I did not feel a connection despite being surrounded by supportive and loving faces I did not feel connected. I felt as if I was walking around alone in a fog.

What became clear is that all tasks seemed to overwhelm me, and nothing I touched seemed to get finished. I just kept reminding myself that despite feeling that I am the only one who can handle things, it is not only acceptable but wise to share the to-do list with my children. So, today I let go.

30

The Others

"It's always inspiring when people all come together and be strong as a group. This is why I feel so strongly to put the message to people that we need to stand together in tough times."
~ Anne-Marie

Growing up, I was taught to be self-sufficient and that depending on another was a sign of weakness. However, through the years, I've learned that you need to be a friend to have a friend. We demonstrate that by showing up when we are needed. Getting older, I have seen the benefit of being there for others and what a privilege it is to show up during difficult times, when someone is hospitalized, or when someone has passed away. I've also not always been the kind of friend I wanted to be, so I've worked hard at being selfless during these times.

However, knowing that this is part of what I have learned, I am still uncomfortable with people showing up for me. I have done everything in my power to keep myself together and not ask for help until a friend approached me and said that I was denying others the opportunity to be a friend to me. Despite being paralyzed by my feelings, I needed to let others show up and be there.

Today I am deeply grateful for that decision. The house was

filled with the others – children, grandchildren, in-laws, and friends. People came in and out of our home, paying their respects and checking on me. Phone calls from friends, co-workers, and family added to the sense of being loved and cared for.

Neighbors came bearing coffee cakes, friends brought home-cooked meals, and co-workers came to blow the autumn leaves off my lawn. These friendships are a blessing. I believe the kindness of others allowed me to enter my new life.

31

The Outfit

"I want my outfit to match my mood."
~ Dakota Johnson

And then it was time to face my closet and find something to wear to the wake and funeral services. I wanted something that wasn't a work outfit and, after looking, felt I did not have anything appropriate to wear.

I was overwhelmed with the prospect of going to a store and just devastated that I even had to look for something. I mustered up some energy and went to a couple of clothing stores. But just being in the store and searching for something started the tears and sent me running back to the parking lot.

I knew that no matter how distraught I felt, I needed to get through this task, so I again entered the store, hoping to find something quickly. But this time, I was approached by the store manager, and she asked how she could help me. I explained that I was looking for something to wear to my husband's funeral and, still crying, went straight to the back of the store, avoiding eye contact.

She grabbed my hand and took me into one of the dressing rooms where she offered to bring a few outfits for me to try. For the next hour, she brought in skirts, blouses, scarves, and jackets until I was able to find something that fit, that I liked, and that felt appropriate for the occasion.

It had been three days since my loved one passed. I was grateful for the kindness and generosity of this stranger. Despite how awful this day had been, I approached the checkout counter feeling a bit lighter.

32

The Salmon Dinner

"Food, to me, is always about cooking and eating
with those you love and care for."
~ David Chang

Four days after my loved one died, I was preparing dinner for my son's wife and in-laws, who had flown in from the west coast. Somehow it felt crucial that I share our home with this part of the family. I couldn't believe they had traveled so far for a family they barely knew. It meant even more to us knowing that our daughter-in-law's mother had made this trip despite battling cancer and being on chemotherapy. The kindness and effort exhibited by this part of our family required that I do something special. For me, there is nothing more special than welcoming someone to your home as the smells of a home-cooked meal greet them at the door.

I grew up in a family where food was central to any gathering and wanted this meal to be remarkable. It would be my first dinner party without my loved one. I started to think about why we were gathered, and the menu came together in a flash. We would have salmon with mustard sauce, garlic asparagus, roasted rosemary potatoes with salad, all because this was my loved one's favorite meal.

Having spent the previous three weeks at the hospital, I realized there was no food in our house, and grocery shopping was a priority. I went to our local specialty market: my mission was to get the freshest produce and salmon for my dinner.

I prepared much of the food in advance and set the table for my guests. The meal was timed so enticing smells floated from our kitchen when the guests arrived. We made some small talk about my husband's paintings and sat down to enjoy the salmon dinner. We ended the dinner with dessert and coffee, and the family left early. We were all emotionally exhausted.

When everyone left, I realized how grateful I was to have been distracted for another day preparing and sharing my loved one's favorite meal. I never told them why this dinner was so important to me, but it was incredible to realize I could still welcome people to our home and share something that had always brought him joy.

33

The Funeral

*"Don't go to the funeral until the day
of the funeral. Live this day."
~ Valerie Harper*

I found myself speeding to the funeral home, knowing that it was an appointment I had to keep. My children met me, and we all climbed into the limousine that was to take us to our beloved's service.

Arriving at the church, I made my way to the front row, noticing the family and friends there. My daughter had selected individuals to speak, read, and share thoughts of my husband and her father. Our children and eldest granddaughter spoke to the mourners. I sat in the front row and was inconsolable, thinking I should have said or done something to contribute. I wanted to tell everyone how much I loved him, how much I missed him, and how truly unique and special he was…but instead, I sat filled with grief and regret.

After the service, the slow procession continued to the cemetery, where added words were shared. The mourners were invited to a small reception, and everyone climbed into their respective cars. However, our limousine took off as if we were in a cops and robbers movie. The driver was speeding so fast that we were literally sliding from one side of the seat to the other. I had gone from deep intense grief to now smiling at the absurdity of our get-away ride.

We quickly arrived at the facility, so I could pay them for their services before any of the invited arrived. The facility was lovely, and the food a bit undercooked, but our family was able to share a meal with our friends. As I walked around to the various tables, thanking people for attending, they joined me with tears or a funny story about my husband.

Looking back on this day, I remember the range of emotions. There was the deep sadness over the loss of my loved one, joy from hearing lovely words about him, the pride over his artwork and po-etry, the absurdity of the limousine ride, shame for not speaking at his service, and enormous relief when the day was finally over. I was a woman on a mission who could now say "mission accomplished," curl up into a ball, and do nothing.

34

The Facebook Posts

*"The thing that we are trying to do at Facebook, is just help
people connect and communicate more efficiently."*
~ Mark Zuckerberg

The day after my loved one passed, my children and some of
our friends posted messages on Facebook informing their groups
that my husband was gone. Some posted messages that he was a
creative genius and prolific artist, spotlighting his unique work.
They shared some instances of his wicked sense of humor. A few of
the older grandchildren wrote that he was a fantastic grandfather,
inspirational, and would be missed. Some of our friends changed
their profile pictures to one of his paintings, or a black and white
photograph he'd taken. A few others posted one of his poems. It
was a wonderful tribute in the social media age.

I, too, participated and posted a message on Facebook informing our family and friends of our loss. I thanked everyone for their
support, words of inspiration, and being a part of our lives. The
problem was that every message I read reminded me that my life's
partner was gone. Every moment I spent on my computer kept me
focused on my loss. So, I begged off of Facebook for a moment,
hoping that no one had mentioned my loved one.

I needed to remember that the posts were, indeed, a tribute to him. These tributes came from his friends' hearts, and those posts enabled me to experience my loved one through their eyes. To see how he had impacted them and how they would miss his company. This is a gift that I will cherish and hold on to as I go through my grief.

35

The Perfect Cards

"God gave you a gift of 84,600 seconds today.
Have you used one of them to say thank you?"
~ William Arthur Ward

Somewhere in my latchkey childhood, I must have seen someone on a television show or read a Dear Abby article that demanded a perfect thank you card be written for an act of kindness. Having this standard of decorum embedded in my consciousness, I knew that even in my most profound moments of grief, there were things that had to be done. I needed to send the 'thank you' cards that mocked me from the end of my dining room table. I would walk by and just stare at them, knowing that whatever I wrote would feel sad, pathetic, and inadequate for the sentiments in my heart.

So, who were these special people I wanted to acknowledge? We had six pallbearers: my son, daughter, son-in-law, and three men who were part of our chosen family. It was essential to recognize these six people because they meant so much to both of us. I felt the pressure. The days passed and, somehow, I kept failing to do this critical task. I wanted to come up with the perfect words and expressions of gratitude. But as days passed, I became more and more unsure of the proper wording.

I sat at my dining room table and invited a kind and loving god to sit with me as I addressed each card. My head told me they were late and not to bother sending them, but my spirit knew differently. As I began writing, I started criticizing my handwriting and my message. I reminded myself that these cards were not supposed to be perfect — they were only meant to express what I felt.

So I picked up my pen and began to write. The handwriting was not pretty, the sentiments in the cards were not as meaningful or as deep as I wanted them to be, but with every card that I wrote, I began to feel a sense of accomplishment. I acknowledged these very important people in my life and am grateful that I could check off one more thing on my list of MUST DOs.

36

The Emotions

"The best way out is always through."
~ Robert Frost

I woke up today, and the moment I opened my eyes, my new reality hit. I never thought I could feel so tired, such despair or this kind of sadness. This sadness swallows me up into nothingness: the place where there is nothing or no one else. I had slept only a few hours. I was, again, a woman on a mission. This time the mission was to get this day over with as quickly as possible. I found myself speeding to the funeral home, knowing that it was an appointment I had to keep. My children met me, and we all climbed into the limousine that was to take us to our beloved's service.

Initially, I thought I would not survive the feelings I was experiencing: the despair, pain, and emptiness that marked my new-found life were nearly unbelievable. My partner of twenty years, eight months, and twenty-four days was gone after a debilitating illness. I was heartbroken, neatly shattered like a piece of safety glass. The word heartbroken had never meant what it now did.

For the first time in my life, I understood the story of married couples who live and die together. You know how one of them dies, and the mate follows shortly behind? I now understood the anguish. Was my loss so painful that the only way through it was to die? I wasn't sure. On some level, I knew it was not-- yet it was perfectly fine with me to die, too.

I knew from past experience that if I could manage stay in the moment, I could get through anything. The struggle occurred whenever my thoughts drifted into some imaginary future. Looking back on this day, I remember the variety of waves: deep sadness over our loss, joy from hearing lovely words shared about him, pride about over his artwork, the absurdity of our wild limousine ride, my shame for not speaking at his service, and the flood of relief when the day was finally over.

My grief was deep, but today I remembered my father's passing and thought of my mother. It's been twelve years since she passed, and I wish I could speak to her. I had been too wrapped up in my own experience to know the depth of her loss. But today I can see I had no idea what she was going through. I also can't presume to understand their season together: it was the sum of the shared experiences that a lifetime together brings. I wish I could just say how truly sorry I am for her loss and that today I do understand. I want her to tell me that I will get through this, that I will be fine, and that I will smile one day again.

Today I have recommitted to allowing my feelings; I won't try to fix them, I will just feel them. I remind myself that even though right now they are painful, not all of my past was. If I could erase those feelings, my memories would go away as well. Some of these memories are what keep me connected to the good.

37

The First Night

"The house seemed so empty without him. And I thought about the life we'd been building together for all that time. I realized I was on the brink of losing it all. It just scared me into reality."
~ Hunter Tylo

Of all the family members, my son stayed the longest. He did a few things around the house, but he showed up and supported me – the most important thing he could. While he was visiting, I tried hard to keep myself together, but in reality, all I wanted was to be alone and cry in private. I felt that I needed to be strong and not show too much heartbreak so he wouldn't leave worried.

But now he was going, and all I wanted was to escape my feelings. I didn't know how I could do that, but my options included screaming, cursing, hitting, staying out all night, gambling, over-eating – anything just not to have to feel. I told myself that I wanted solitude just to grieve in the quiet of my newfound widowhood, but the reality was that I wanted to isolate, to escape, and make my feelings just go away.

The unhealthy coping behaviors that surfaced the most in this first year were overspending, overeating, overworking, and, occasionally, gambling. But when I was almost overwhelmed, gambling went to the head of the list. What made it even worse was recognizing that I shouldn't be gambling away the money I had set aside to take care of myself. Sometimes, I could reach out and keep myself busy by sharing an evening with a friend.

Knowing that my son had left, a friend invited me to join her for coffee with a group of friends. I met her there, but I felt uncomfortable and obsessed with keeping my feelings under wraps. People were welcoming. They were generous with their hugs and kind words. It wasn't long before I knew I'd be escaping to the casino. Leaving the group early, I couldn't get there fast enough. I gambled all night. The problem with trying to escape is that eventually, everyone has to go home. There is no escaping this grief.

As the sun came up, I drove home quietly, and it hit me that I didn't want to return to a house filled with funeral memorabilia. It no longer was the home we had shared – now it was my house. I was filled with dread. Worst of all, I felt ashamed. I did not know what to do. So, I cried and cried, and in between the sobs, I asked the god of my understanding for help to get me through this first night.

But, if I'm rigorously honest, just like with my anger and bitterness, there were times I didn't want to stop myself, so I simply didn't call friends. Instead, I would gamble all night and, eventually, come home feeling broken.

I wish I could share that my home felt like home right away, but it did not. Grieving is a process, and it continues. I know that I am better just because I look forward to coming home again.

38

The Silence

"Listen to the silence. Listen to your life. Be present, not just think about what's going on next week, next month."
~ Mike Dirnt

Before my loved one's passing, there were always sounds in the house. The sounds came from the television and stereo as he only slept a few hours at a time. There was a constant low murmur from the oxygen concentrator, which continuously delivered filtered and compressed air. Then there were sounds from the nebulizer treatments to help improve his lung function. And finally, the horrible raspy, drowning sounds that his compromised lungs made when he lay down.

Then one day, there was only silence. I turned off the television and stereo, the air compressor was returned to the medical supply store, and the nebulizers were thrown in the trash. Initially, I welcomed the silence. However, as the days passed, I found myself dreading it. It became clear that the new silence meant that how we had lived the last three years of his life would only be a memory. A terrible memory. My loved one had passed and left behind a deafening silence.

During the day, the lack of noise drove me to look around the house for something to do. I was so scattered I couldn't concentrate, so I would just sit and wait for the day to pass. The evening silence brought its challenges. I got anxious and unable to identify what I was feeling. The evenings dragged on, providing me with plenty of time to contemplate his passing and see how alone I really was.

As I sit in my three-season room, I see a pair of deer nibbling on ferns at the edge of the tree line. I realize that if there had been a lot of noise, the deer would not have come onto the property, and I would not have been able to appreciate just how beautiful this moment is. So today, this hour and this moment, I welcome the silence.

39

The Grief Books

"On the floor by my bed, there are heaps of books I want to read,
books I have to read, and books I believe I need to read."
~ Karl Ove Knausgard

Returning home from the store, I stopped at the top of my driveway to retrieve the mail accumulated for the last few days. I came into the house, dropped the stack on the dining room table, and went about my business. Later I noticed that this seemed to be a new habit I was developing – the table had several stacks of mail. I had looked through absolutely none of them.

That evening I decided it was time to sort through the materials and see if there was anything I needed to deal with. I discovered that most stacks were filled with junk mail, newspapers, and magazines. However, there were several bills and, to my amazement, a few books. The books were about grief and were written specifically for someone who had experienced a recent loss.

The books on my table had been mailed or dropped off by friends and family members who thought that being a recent widow demanded that I read these books. I'm sure they hoped that whatever insight I gained would help me deal with my grief. However, as I started reading, it became clear that I wasn't retaining any information. I kept trying to read, but I noticed that I had turned several pages and didn't remember a word. Something that had always brought me pleasure was now an issue – I couldn't even escape the pain by reading.

I could not concentrate long enough to absorb the contents of the books, but instead, what occurred to me is the reminder that I have some fantastic friends. They thought beyond themselves to try to help me through one of the most painful periods of my life.

They were beyond thoughtful and generous and, even though I could not read the stack of books at that moment, I decided to move them to my end table. I know that, as with everything else in life, this too will pass. One day I will be lost in the words on those pages and will be able to concentrate long enough to reap the benefits from the books I have been given.

40

The Insane Thoughts

"God has blessed me with an amazing family, friends, and work colleagues that have been my joy, my support, and my sanity. I don't know what I'd do without them."
~ Josie Loren

Since my loved one passed, I have been depressed, somewhat suicidal, erratic, angry, weepy, disoriented, and riddled with self-pity. I began questioning my sanity and knew I had to look at my behavior. because I did not accept that any of it came from grief.

Several from my circle of support assured me this insanity actually did stem from grief. But hearing it didn't change a thing. My husband had only been gone for a handful of days, and, as crazy as my insides felt, I appeared to others as if nothing had changed. That stoic outside image protected me from the weakness and vulnerability in my heart.

In the past, such weakness spurred me to seek a god. That effort provided me with the strength to cope. But I now questioned whether any god could help me. This felt very different, much harder, and completely overwhelming. I wanted to believe that this greater power could get through and provide some relief. These feelings brought me to my knees, and the only thing I knew to do was pray.

I prayed for the ability to survive all this discomfort. I knew it wouldn't be easy, but I had hope. Despite feeling insane with grief, I had to begin by simply trusting that the god of my understanding would take care of me again.

Thirty-nine days since the loss of my beloved husband, and I believe that a loving god has given me a reprieve from my thinking. I have made small steps in reaching out to others for support and have started to pray for an open mind so I can hear the hope they offer. My hope is simple: I just want to survive one more day. Glimpses of sanity return, and I notice alternate options for managing feelings of despair.

Nothing had prepared me for the thoughts stemming from my grief and sadness. They showed up when I least expected them, bombarding me with painful images and gut-wrenching knots that contaminated the present and ruined any potential future.

I had become afraid of what my future held, and the unknown was causing anxiety. I didn't know what to expect. When my thoughts found me, I was afraid, my heart raced, and the beginning of a panic attack was not far behind. All of this because I didn't know how to fix my life. I had no clue what to do next, and there was the ever-pressing question of "how would I take care of myself?" Given that I had been the sole care-giver for our family, this was a sure sign of just how distorted my thoughts had become.

So instead of focusing on the future, I attempted to stay in my present batting away my fear like flies. I focused on the here and now, stopped ruminating over past losses, or worrying about what my future held.

Every day I woke up remembering that my loved one was dead. It's a horrible way to start the day, and it seemed to reinforce the worry that this overwhelming grief would never go away. Remembering his death set the tone for the rest of the day, the insufferable gloom of new life.

One day I decided to start my day without bereavement as

my first thought. I tried to find solutions that would spare me that daily wake-up call. I tried praying the moment I opened my eyes or reading some spiritual materials to sidestep the feelings of loss and pain.

But I know the only way to get through a feeling is to feel it. There is no escape. There was no way to circumvent my grief. It occurred to me that perhaps I needed to ask my friends for some ideas on a way to get a better start on the day. One close friend suggested I pray for peace and focus on my gratitude. I did. It's strange that in the middle of my grief, I could still experience gratitude and recognize that I am grateful to be able to feel gratitude. I set a goal is to remember that being in the present brings the only emotional relief I can count on. I strive to focus on this present where I am OK. I have people who love me and, most importantly, people I love. Today I have the strength to loosen my grip on fear and focus on the good in my life.

I began to participate in an email gratitude list. I listed everything from my health to the moments of peace I have had. The serenity I started to feel was only possible because of the trust I have in my spiritual community and my willingness to try what they suggest. Even though I still wake up remembering I have been widowed, that email helps change my focus and sets the tone for a more positive day.

41

The Support

"It's very hard to find true friends when your life is a bumpy ride full of twists and turns. But, I'm glad that amidst all the ramblings in my life I have managed to win some great friends."
~ *Harbhajan Singh*

After my loved one's death, I was so grateful that they came – children, grandchildren, son-in-law, daughter-in-law, old and new friends, and coworkers. Some marched right in as if on a mission, while others waited and stood back and watched.

- They came to help make funeral arrangements as I was almost catatonic.
- They came to bring food so I wouldn't have to cook.
- They came to hold me and let me cry.
- They came to drop off flowers.
- They came to move furniture.
- They came to clean my porch, my yard, and to blow the autumn leaves into the woods.
- They came to take me to my support group.
- They came to restore my library and move his art studio back to the basement.

- They came to sort through clothes.
- They came to stack and re-stack wood for the fireplace.
- They came to paint.
- They came from around the corner and from other states.
- They came to take me to dinner.
- They came to keep me company.
- They came to share their tears with me.
- They came, they came, and they continued to come.

I am so grateful that they did. This is important for me to remember because feeling so desperately hopeless, it has been too easy to see myself as a victim drowning in self-pity. If I let myself go into these feelings, I deny everything that my life experiences have taught me.

During this time of grief, the greatest gift I have is remembering that the antidote for my self-pity is gratitude. So, for today I am grateful to have nurtured the relationships with these absolutely exceptional people who took time out of their lives to show up for mine.

42

The Spiritual Principles

"Spiritual principles do not change, but we do."
~ Marianne Williamson

As an adult, I continually strive to become a better person and have made an effort through the years to search for a more meaningful path than the one I had been living. Through the years, I felt a void. I tried to fill the emptiness by reading spiritual materials and dabbling in several religions. Eventually, I settled into being a better human by finding a spiritual mentor and learning to live according to spiritual principles.

These principles were seeds that provided hope when life was complicated and felt unmanageable. They brought courage when facing adversity and the love that enables us to take one step forward when we want to hide in bed. Living these principles had, many times, provided me with strength. However, since my husband's death, I found that while I might use them to treat you better, I often managed to forget that they also applied to me.

These principles are the foundation of what makes me – me. My character, my integrity, and my self-compassion were at stake. In my heart, I believed that I needed to focus on the principles of surrender, honesty, hope. I needed faith for change and growth to happen. I began to question my life and my purpose. I was only existing, and part of me wanted more. I needed to look at what I was doing and how I was reacting to the events in my life, no matter how painful they were.

My day was structured to avoid my feelings by obsessively working, binge-watching TV, and not allowing any time for reflection or thought. By taking a look, I found that my life was unmanageable because of all the feelings that I was trying to avoid. I needed to surrender the avoidance to begin processing my grief.

I made a conscious effort to remind myself that I wasn't alone and that others had found some solace by being honest about their feelings. I also knew that an open mind, considering suggestions made by spiritual mentors, and willingness to try something different played a part. I chose to believe in their experiences, and my hope grew. I understood that if I applied the same principles to my grief that I, too, could find the peace I craved.

I have chosen to lean on my faith, trust that my grief will eventually become manageable, and my faith will likely strengthen. Until that time, I hang onto the spiritual principles of surrender, hope, and honesty as I continue to turn to a god that loves me.

43

The Clothes

*"I am a complete sentimentalist when it comes to clothes. I have so
many memories attached to them that I can't throw anything out."*
~ *Vanessa Paradis*

After his death, I was overwhelmed with his things. Trying to
decide what was to go and what was to stay. His closet and bureau
drawers were filled with everything from shirts and trousers to belts
and ties. There were even dirty clothes in the laundry basket that
had to be washed, folded, and stacked. I did not know what I was
to do with them.

Most of the clothes had no meaning but took up space in the
closet and my mind. Twenty-six days since my loved one passed, a
friend came to assist me in sorting through his clothes. Most of the
clothes were donated to charitable organizations, but a few things
were given to close friends and family.

I kept a few special things, articles of clothing associated with
the happy moments that had filled our lives. His University of New
Mexico sweatshirt with the Lobos logo reminded him of s as a
great runner. It reminded me of the joy in his voice when he spoke
of those days. He loved that sweatshirt, and so did I. The painting
aprons brought back memories of a time he was physically able to

91

work. That brought joy to us both so, I kept two of them. I even left his ratty bathrobe hanging behind the bathroom door. I wasn't ready to part with it. For now the bathrobe doesn't have to go anywhere. It still belongs behind the door and in my life.

The removal of clothing is very personal. Some people choose to keep everything, others thin some things out, and some get rid of everything. For me, those special items kept me connected to him in a significant way. There are no rules about what goes or what stays. Each of us must decide what works best for our situation, remembering that once the clothes are gone, there's no bringing them back.

44

The Bitter and the Shame

*"We're often afraid of looking at our shadow because
we want to avoid the shame or embarrassment that
comes along with admitting mistakes."*
~ Marianne Williamson

You never know when love will find you, and for me, it was when I met my husband. He was forty-four, and I was thirty-eight years old. We decided to get married and attempted to blend our families. He had two sons and a daughter and I brought one son to the mix.

Of his three, I was privileged to become close to his daughter. Her outgoing nature and ability to embrace all of us with open arms was one of the reasons we were a successful blended family. However, within 30 days of my husband's death I felt betrayed by an incident involving her.

On the telephone, we both said things in anger. I know I wasn't sorry and don't believe she was either. However, immediately after that phone call, I crawled into a grief-stricken protective shell, feeling like we would never be a family again.

Several months later, I continued to stumble through my life under a cloud. The darkness around me seemed impenetrable, and I wore the badges of self-pity, intolerance and anger on my chest as if they were medals to be proud of. Without even noticing, I nurtured this darkness and grew many negative traits and flaws from it.

As time passed, I found myself unable to reach out. I was already in a great deal of pain and feared that the damage would be irrevocable if we spoke. Understanding that, I would have lost both my husband and my only daughter if nothing was done, I knew it was time to reach out. I reached deep into my heart, looking for the right words, and picked up the phone to salvage whatever relationship was left. Feeling beyond vulnerable, I asked my god to help me find the right words. I knew I could not talk about anything going on with me, but I did want to check on her and her family.

It took me almost three months to pick up the phone inquiring about how everyone was doing. It made a difference. Even though the telephone calls at first were short and seemed forced, it became clear that not causing additional harm allowed each of us to begin healing, to let go of the ugly incident, and to start supporting each other through our individual grief.

45

The List

"My to-do list is so long that it doesn't have an end;
it has an event horizon."
~ Craig Bruce

I still wasn't prepared for the anxiety I felt when I needed to make a "To Do" as a widow. Choosing to make this list despite my feelings gave me a momentary reprieve. I was doing something that felt productive. My list began with the people and institutions that needed to be informed that my love of twenty years was no longer with me. I knew some things had to be taken care of, whether or not I thought they mattered.

My list began with the Social Security Administration. They would now discontinue his benefits and issue their absurd $255 final check for funeral expenses.

Next on my list were my supervisor and the Human Resource department. It had only been a few days since my husband's service, and the thought of having to listen to anyone saying how sorry they were made me want to avoid the call. I only had five bereavement days, and they needed to know when I would be returning to work. I was barely functional and had decided to use vacation days or file for short-term disability but was not yet ready to commit to either one. The only thing I knew was expecting someone to come to terms with the death of a partner in five days is absurd.

Our bank and credit card companies were next on my list. They needed to know of my husband's passing so his credit cards could be canceled. I also needed to inform his physicians of his passing to cancel previously scheduled appointments.

Looking around my house, I realized that there was only one call I was looking forward to making: the durable medical equipment company. There were oxygen tanks, a concentrator and hoses all over the house. The sooner these things were removed, the better.

Making this list enabled me to start to face my new reality. Even in grief, life goes on, and with that, some things must be taken care of. The sooner I could make the calls, the sooner my new life would start to show itself to me. So, I picked up the telephone and placed my first call.

46

The Shrink

*"Your grief path is yours alone, and no one else can walk it,
and no one else can understand it."*
~ Terri Irwin.

A few days after my loved one passed, I again reached out to
the psychiatrist. I had various complaints: unimaginable grief, depression, forgetfulness, and the inability to sleep or eat. I was filled
with anxiety over my imminent return to work and worried that
I would not be able to function at my high-stress job. After some
discussion, it became apparent he didn't believe that I was ready to
return to work. He submitted the paperwork required for short-
term disability.

Part of me was relieved that I would stay home to try to put
my new life together. But the other part of me was ruthless with
constant thoughts of not being good enough, showing weakness,
and judging myself as if this loss was a small thing. I had to remember that the loss of my partner, friend, husband, and lover was
a big damned deal. And that adjusting to it in five days, like my
bereavement benefit, was not even a possibility.

Returning home from the appointment, I was very aware that I
needed to allow my feelings of grief to just be. Glancing at the date

for my next appointment and knowing that steps were being taken on my short-term disability application, I felt less stressed. I was able to let out a sigh of relief as I didn't think I could pretend to convince anyone, especially myself, that I was okay. I began to hope that having some extra time at home would help me heal.

47

The Bang

"You have to forget about the bad memories and push on."
~ Tammy Abraham

Since my loved one's death, I found it difficult to go to bed. The anticipation that sleep would elude me one more night caused anxiety. I often thought about and relived the trauma of my husband's emergencies. I found myself incapable of turning those memories off.

The nighttime was especially difficult; there were so many instances where he struggled with his health at night. There seemed to be something that made the evening crises much harder to handle than if the same situation occurred during the daytime. Perhaps it was because we were both trying to settle in for the night, maybe the fact that we were tired, or just being awakened from a deep sleep to a full-blown emergency. It doesn't matter why I developed this feeling – all that I know is I continued to struggle with the night.

One evening I was particularly grappling with sleep and, when I finally did, I was awakened by a horrible bang. He had collapsed again, and I ran upstairs to help. As I turned the corner to the bathroom, I realized that it couldn't be him: he had died. I turned on the light and saw that the mirror over the sink had fallen to the floor. To my amazement, it had not broken. I, on the other hand, was shaking, crying, and remembering the many times he had collapsed in this very room.

The memories are fresh, and conditioned by years of crisis, I responded as if his life depended on it. I needed to heal and move on from this. I recognized my strengths, and one of them is a knack for honest self-appraisal. I was suffering from the trauma caused by living many years in crisis mode. In my heart, I knew that this would require professional help. I trust that making this decision will lead to a healthier existence.

48

War is Hell

*"The thing about post-traumatic stress disorder, we know about
one in five, about 20 percent of individuals that are exposed to a
direct traumatic stress will develop this disorder."
~ Dale Archer*

I wasn't alive for WWI or WWII to have experienced shell
shock or combat fatigue. I was never in combat, so experiencing the
intense feelings of impending doom, anger, or hyper-vigilance is
disconcerting. Memories attack me, and I am never truly aware of
what will set them off. When things are quiet, I experience recur-
ring flashbacks of specific hospitalizations or significant illness at
our home.

Sleep was challenging as I tried to keep the memories of
oxygen concentrators and life support machines out of my dreams.
Crying spells occurred for no apparent reason, and I found myself
avoiding places associated with bad memories. I felt different and
alone, but my inner core knew this was not true. I began to understand and recognize the symptoms that I was experiencing were
more than grief – that I was suffering from post-traumatic stress
disorder.

My mind contains twenty years of traumatic memories. I can

describe the hospital stays, every stressful moment, outbursts (his and mine), and all the accompanying feelings that went with that experience. I'd put on my brave face, deal with whatever life dealt us but afterward, once things settled down and he returned home, I would plummet into depression.

I am a ruthless critic. I've become highly skilled at passing judgment on myself for feelings of hopelessness and fear, being uncomfortable and avoiding people in hospitals. In other words, for being human. Allowing compassion to enter my heart, I see that anyone who had experienced twenty years of endless crises would be traumatized. I need more support than I get from a grief group. I need to see a mental health professional with post-traumatic stress disorder expertise. I ended my day by calling my old therapist to refer me to a PTSD specialist, as I believed this would be another big step on my path to healing.

49

The Caregiver

*"Caregiving has no second agendas or hidden motives.
The care is given from love for the joy of giving without
expectation, no strings attached."*
~ Gary Zukav

The loss of my loved one profoundly changed my life: he was gone, and the emptiness that threatened to swallow me made me inconsolable. But what had changed? I still had a good job, a lovely home, the love of children, grandchildren, and friends, but the thing that made me the 'most me I had ever been' was gone. After many years, my role as a caregiver had also gone and left me with more time, more emptiness and no idea how to fill my days. The expert caregiver didn't have anyone to care for. Eventually, I realized that was not true. When I glanced at my life, I made an important discovery: I had to care for myself.

I'd spent so many years doing for him that doing for me was a foreign concept. Looking at my current situation, I needed to start with the small things. The basics. I had to make sure that I was eating healthily and regularly. I needed to organize my house to serve my needs instead of the needs of my now-dead husband. I needed to make time for sleep and not stay up most of the night until exhaustion hit me.

Once I had mastered basic survival (food, sleep, organization), I began to look at bigger things. It was time to tend to some of my unmet needs. To start caring for myself, I had to make appointments: it had been many years since I'd had a physical, a mammogram, a bone density exam, or been seen by a dentist. I had to work to change my patterns of isolation – part of me felt ready to reconnect with friends and family. I felt a need to return to participation in my community, so I began to look for some sort of commitment that would get me out of my self-centeredness.

The things I had done so freely for him, without regard for my own health, my lack of sleep, or my fear I turned out to be the things I needed to start doing for myself. The steps for self-care were small at first, and they consisted of reaching out to friends who had been there for us, answering the phone when it rang, allowing others to be kind to me, and picking up the telephone to make those essential physicians appointments. I committed to showing up for my life with the dedication and love I had shown for him. By doing this, my new life started to emerge.

50

Nighttime Hours

*"Early to bed and early to rise makes a man
healthy, wealthy, and wise."*
~ Benjamin Franklin

Several years before my dear one died, his compromised lungs made it impossible for him to sleep lying down. The recliner chair gave him a better position, so we moved into the living room. In an attempt to maintain some closeness, I began sleeping on the chaise on the other side of the room.

The nighttime hours brought challenges that we tried to manage and control. The medications he needed to open his airways only allowed one or two consecutive hours of sleep. He tried to keep busy working on his computer with the stereo or television on in the background. I found it difficult to sleep because of the constant noise. Of course, when it was quiet, I would wake up in a panic to see that he was still breathing.

The first couple of weeks after his passing, I was so exhausted that I would collapse into a dead sleep. But once everyone was gone sleep continued to be a challenge. My friends recommended everything from taking a hot bath, drinking tea, reading a book, or using prayer and meditation to provide my mind with the quiet it desperately needed. I eliminated the hot bath idea as I don't like them, and hot tea was not something I enjoyed. I tried reading but couldn't concentrate long enough to retain anything. Keeping an open mind, I started to use prayer and meditation in the hope that I could quiet my mind enough to fall to sleep. So far, it hasn't worked.

I dreaded the nighttime hours. Even though the house was quiet, I just couldn't turn off the sounds in my head. The terrible sounds of the oxygen concentrator, nebulizers, and the noise from his lungs replayed. Eventually, I turned to something I'd seen work: noise.

I began to sleep with either music or the television on; they helped me drift away to as good a night's sleep as I could muster. I knew this was a temporary solution, but I'm starting to have a little faith that whatever I need to get to the next day will be provided. Tonight I listen to some classical music until I fade away.

51

The Healing Heart

"Being able to give someone a hug from the heart,
it's healing. It's healing for yourself and healing for
others, and we need a lot of that."
~ Big Show

After my beloved passed, I was trying to figure out what I needed to do to get past the pain I felt. My goal was to come up with a plan to bypass the pain. I learned there is no ignoring the loss of a loved one.

The simple truth is that reminders of our life together were constant and in plain sight. Walk by my loved one's office, drive past his favorite restaurant, or invite someone to use my extra theatre ticket. Twenty years married, his passing affected every area of my life. The realization that I felt pain whenever I was reminded of my loss has demanded that I fearlessly search for the path to healing. It was just so big and overwhelming.

Avoiding heartbreak hadn't worked. Every time I turned a corner, I ran into an emotional brick wall. I found that all my energy was placed on fixing these unrelenting feelings by prioritizing healing. As I dug deeper, I discovered that I was also trying to fix anything and everything that made me uncomfortable. Often, I was unaware of the discomfort I felt until after I had overeaten or binge-watched an entire season of some television show.

The day's question was always, 'how do I get through these feelings?' I began by praying for the ability to deal with my emotions. I learned that I cannot bypass a feeling no matter how much I want to.

One day, it occurred to me that I had been praying for the wrong thing. I needed to ask for the courage to feel my grief, disappointment, or just loneliness. I had been so wrapped up in trying to fix these feelings that it never occurred to me that all I needed to do was to feel them. Perhaps with less energy spent fighting them, I could get through my grief, and the healing of my heart could begin.

There is no quick way to heal from the pain of a broken heart. It seems fitting that the pain I felt seemed as big as the love I had felt. I had to trust that I would get to where I needed to go by truly honoring and trusting my feelings.

52

The Corner and His Chair

*"I think a lot of us can relate to not choosing to face a painful
memory, and something that's a painful past,
and wanting to pretend like it never happened."*
~ Derek Magyar

Four years before my loved one passed, he began experiencing
difficulty breathing when lying down. Our solution to this situation
was searching for the perfect chair – his recliner. It needed to be
comfortable so he could sleep but practical to continue to work on
his computer. These were the guidelines we used to hunt for the
perfect chair.

When the chair arrived, I arranged the living room keeping in
mind that he needed to use his computer, printer, and oxygen and
have easy access to the rest of the house. I found the perfect spot
and centered the chair between the two front windows near the
corner of the room. This is where he spent the next four years.

When he died, I avoided looking at that side of the room and
the equipment there. But with just a little effort, his chair was
removed, the oxygen concentrator returned, and his computer relo-
cated to his office. The uncomfortable feeling stayed. The profound
emptiness of him not sitting, sleeping, or working in that corner of

the room was a constant reminder of my loss.

Being solution-oriented, I moved the furniture around, bought new decorator pillows, and attempted to make that side of the room cozy. It looked nice but wasn't enough to remove my discomfort or erase my memories. I would lie on the couch to watch television, and my eyes would wander to the corner. At the end of the day, I would lie on the chaise and try to close my eyes but would find myself again looking at the corner where he had lived his life.

How do you wipe away years of memories by just moving the furniture and putting a plant on an end table? You don't. I still avoid looking toward that corner of my living room and imagine a time when I won't be so sensitive to those memories. All I needed to do in the moment was feel the uncomfortableness, embrace the change, and pray to get through this next part of my sorrow just by living day-to-day.

53

The Great Escape

"I don't go out to parties because I'd look terrible in pictures.
My escape is television – it's like meditation to me."
~ Alber Elbaz

Before my loved one passed, the television was continuously on as the background noise of his life. He'd watch shows, listen to the music channels, or have it barely audible while he wrote, painted/created, and even slept. I would complain about how insane this was to no avail.

Since his death, the television has been present in every moment. Life showed up in full force, and I needed a break. I was doing exactly what he did – except there was no one here to complain about my behavior. The numbing from my television was a welcome reprieve from crying.

I now watched different shows, but I got lost in the sound. I switched from too violent or realistic to comedies and music. Even though the escape seemed to help me avoid thinking and feeling, I understood that I couldn't do this forever, so I tried to balance my escapism with phone calls to friends, meeting members of my spiritual community, or attending therapy. When I reach out to others in my good moments, I don't have to find them right away.

111

I know that it is the act of reaching out that moves me back toward wholeness.

Continuing to channel-surf and look for mindless entertainment to avoid my feelings reminds me that I am not okay. But today, I commit to doing one bit of self-care: I will write. I pull out a journal and let my thoughts spill onto the paper.

54

The Trust

"Basically, there are two paths you can walk: faith or fear.
It's impossible to simultaneously trust God and not trust God."
~ Charles Stanley

Trust is a funny thing. I've always struggled with deciding who I can trust. Still, the years have taught me that it begins with deciding just to try. Of course, the other person could hurt me. So, I learned to wait and, if my confidence wasn't betrayed, I deemed that person trustworthy. But how does that work with God?

After three horrific weeks in ICU watching the love of my life suffer and die, the question in the back of my mind was, "can I trust the god in my life?" I had given up all thoughts that my husband would get through this alive, but the suffering he faced was unconscionable. And there was nothing I could do to help. The persistent question was, "what kind of a god would do this?" This was a big deal. Huge. It had been difficult for me to connect with a Higher Power. I sure didn't want to get involved with the one I had met as a child.

Yet all of a sudden, the punishing god from my childhood reappeared. This god played a specific role in people's lives and could either rescue or abandon them. Because of my upbringing and early adulthood, I felt challenged to find a god I could have faith in. Eventually, and with practice, I could foster a relationship with what became a kind and loving god.

Were we abandoned by my god? I focused on what my faith had become and what it meant to me. What I know in my heart is that we were neither rescued nor abandoned: we had simply walked through one of life's difficult moments.

I am still haunted by what we went through every day. It was painful and disappointing. I knew none of it could be changed. Much of what I witnessed was unimaginable, but I got through it by constantly praying and sharing my fears with a kind and loving god.

For sixty-five days after my loved one passed, I had spent most of each day sharing my grief with this deity. I do not believe that my god had anything to do with my husband's illness, suffering, or death. I have decided to continue to walk my path in faith. This continues to be a process; the only way I know to have a life where I'm not paralyzed with grief is to do what I have learned – trust my kind and loving God.

55

The Love

"Love is that condition in which the happiness of another person is essential to your own."
~ Robert A. Heinlein

It seems that it has only been a minute since my loved one passed, and the thoughts that I cherish are the moments we shared in love. Not every moment we shared together in the twenty years was easy; however, there was a lot of love. Despite all the moments of uncertainty, fear, illness, ingratitude, and lack of faith, I understand today that our love is what made those difficult moments bearable.

I sometimes worry that all of the difficulties his ill health brought will prevent me from remembering. I think of the many things I did so he would feel loved and know such things weren't done for acknowledgment. I didn't do them to brag that I was a great wife. I did them because I was selfish. I did them so I could experience the reward of the smile that came to his face when a box of oil paints arrived via mail. I craved the look of contentment he had when he smelled the chocolate chip cookies baking.

Now that he is gone, I want to know how I can hold on to those moments of happiness and love we felt. How can I hold on to them when all I feel is pain and sorrow?

The people in my life reminded me to share my grief and not stuff my feelings. They said the feelings of loss and pain would decrease. I hold this thought close to my heart. I try to begin my days by committing to myself that I will continue to share my story and my sadness until I get to the other side and I can once again feel the love.

56

The First Holiday

*"Be thankful for what you have; you'll end up having more.
If you concentrate on what you don't have,
you will never, ever have enough."*
~ Oprah Winfrey

Thanksgiving was around the corner. It was my first widowed holiday. People around me talked over their plans. I kept a low profile and avoided the conversations. I kept myself busy with the minutiae of my day-to-day existence, but there was no escaping this holiday.

Since the loss of my father, Thanksgiving had not been a great time of year for me. Obviously, this year was far worse because my partner was gone. I desperately wanted to avoid all discussions of cooking or where I would be. I wanted the day to come and go with the least amount of intrusion into my life. I couldn't escape the conversations. Everywhere I went, people were discussing their plans. As I made my way around town, holiday decorations were in full display in the stores and on the streets. Even as I sat in front of the television, the Macy's Thanksgiving Day parade commercial seemed to be on at least once every hour.

I knew I was depressed and focused on the darkness in my life:

my husband was deceased, my children lived out of state, and I didn't feel connected with anyone or anything. However, I remembered what this holiday is about, and for most of us, it is about family and gratitude. I knew how blessed I was as several friends and co-workers reached out with invitations to be with their families and share in their feasts. People made an effort to make me feel a part of, so I wouldn't be alone, which touched me.

Thanksgiving arrived, and I told my friends and co-workers that I had accepted an invitation for dinner at a relative's home. Instead, I just stayed home, watched the Macy's parade, and made a small meal. I spent the day stoking the fire and giving myself permission to just hang out and feel whatever I was supposed to be feeling. As my day ended, I gave thanks for the truly wonderful people in my life. I focused on trying to be comfortable in my own skin, and when all was said and done, I was genuinely grateful for my decision to just stay home and be.

57

The Bills

*"If you're able to pay your bills, you pay your bills.
It's as simple as that."*
~ Dave Ramsey

One day my task was simply to see if my automatic deposit had made its way into my checking account. It didn't matter that I was grieving: our financial obligations were still there and needed to be taken care of. It was time to pay our bills.

My loved one was an artist with the brain and organizational style to match. I was more of a pragmatist. I arrogantly thought I was better off than other widows because, throughout our marriage, I had handled the money. I dealt with the credit cards, checking accounts, looked at our investments, and paid our bills.

As I sat down to pay bills, I realized that I was not the same person I was thirty-three days before. Turned out I was more like all the other widows than I suspected: distracted, in pain, and stumbling through these first days of a new life. The extent of my distraction became apparent when it took me twice the time it usually did to access and pay our bills. However, there was a payoff: I felt a little bit normal, almost as if this small act brought back my life as it was before.

I was surprised a few weeks later when I received a late notice from my car loan company. I instantly became indignant: I knew it had been paid.

I pulled out my computer, went to the site, and stared at the screen in disbelief: I could see that I had not, in fact, made the payment. A feeling of impending doom set in: were there other bills I had missed? I searched my computer and found a few other missed statements. They, too, would be late. Trying to be responsible and protect my credit, I knew I needed to fix this ASAP. I placed a few calls and explained the circumstances to our creditors. They were all very kind and promised that the misstep would not affect my credit.

I was starting to grasp the depth of my emotional impairment. I have become grateful to see my limitations and believe that they are temporary.

58

The Holiday Cards

"Give back in some way. Always be thoughtful of others."
~ Jackie Joyner-Kersee

My husband had many gifts, one of them being his artistic ability. Knowing this, I would start bugging him in late October so we – well, really, he – could start designing our card for the upcoming holidays. I had grown accustomed to him creating some very lovely, unique, and at times irreverent cards. The cards ranged from a takeoff on Beavis and Butthead to him spending hours photographing our decorated dining room table and turning it into a masterpiece. His health was always the determining factor. But on this day, what comes to mind is what turned out to be the last card he ever designed. It was simple with a navy-blue background with multiple white spiritual symbols on the cover and Peace on Earth as the message inside. It is still my favorite.

December came. I would normally be addressing envelopes but not that year. He was really gone. I did not have a personal artist to create a card, and frankly, was not in any kind of holiday spirit to buy cards to send. Whatever joy or happiness had usually accompanied the holidays was buried with him. But time doesn't stand still, and even though I did not send any cards, I started to receive them.

The theme seemed to be the same throughout: instead of reflecting holiday joy, they were more like condolence cards. They acknowledged that the holidays would be difficult, that he was physically gone, and it would be a hard adjustment. They even commented that he was special and would be missed. All I could think about was that this was the last freaking thing I wanted to see in my holiday cards. I did not need – or want – another dose of reality.

What could I do with this? How could I turn it around? My experience has taught me that I can stay with this feeling and be angry... but I also know that holding on to any feeling is a choice. I said a quick prayer that helped me restart my day and focus on the kindness and compassion of everyone who bothered to send a card. They took time out of their busy lives to send something to me. I know it must have been hard to write a meaningful message to a recent widow. At that moment, I chose to focus on how blessed I truly am to have these individuals in my life.

.

59

The Appointments

"I have to take care of myself. It's about self-preservation."
~ *Danielle de Niese*

I woke up and realized I didn't feel well. I was nursing a sore throat and a slight fever. It would officially be winter in a couple of days, and it was forty-two degrees outside. The chill in the living room compelled me to drag some wood into the house and start a fire. I bundled up on the couch debating my choices: go to an urgent care center, contact a physician, or just drink some fluids. Then I remembered that I didn't have a personal physician. I had neglected my health and anything related to self-care for many years.

For twenty years, the priority had been to tend to my loved one's healthcare needs. They were many. Managing this complex web of medical conditions required extensive organization and occasional manipulation. I made appointments with cardiology, rheumatology, and pulmonology. I scheduled bloodwork and transported my patient to treatments and infusions. I arranged for nursing care, oxygen delivery and made multiple trips to the pharmacy to pick up multiple medications.

But that day, I sat in my living room debating my next move. I decided to give it another day. If I continued to feel awful, I would go to an urgent care facility near my home. However, it became clear that I needed to begin to care for myself the way I had so meticulously cared for him.

My return to self-care journey began with making a list of the personal healthcare mandates I had neglected: obtaining a primary care physician, scheduling a mammogram and bone density scan, baseline bloodwork, and finally, a dentist. I pulled out my computer to see what providers were available through my insurance plan. I became determined to do things differently. Picking up the telephone, I took action on the decision to love and care for myself. It began right then.

60

The Gift

"When a gift is difficult to give away, it becomes even more rare and precious, somehow gathering a part of the giver to the gift itself."
~ *Cate Blanchett*

My loved one spent the last year of his life making art. He dealt with his illness and his life by writing and painting obsessively. He interpreted life through oils on a canvas or the meticulous writing and sketches on his computer.

Knowing his life was coming to an end, he wrote poetry. It was personal and profound, exposing his innermost thoughts. He was determined to leave something of himself behind. He created beautiful abstract digital artwork on his precious Mac and, when able, painted with his oils. Before his death, he put together a book of his poetry and included some of his artwork. Initially, we ordered five copies with the thought of printing more and perhaps selling them.

However, he passed away shortly after we had ordered his book, and now, I had five copies of this very personal, unique, and final book. It would mean something only to the people who loved him, so I had to take special care to ensure that I gave it to the most suitable ones.

So, on the first Christmas, I sat and started to make a list of people who would appreciate this extraordinary gift. After carefully reviewing the book, I felt it truly captured his essence. It meant showing his obsession, memories, sense of humor, dedication, talent, and love. Because of this, I felt a special obligation to handle this part of his legacy carefully. The final list included his three children and two close friends.

Wrapping the books and writing notes for this unique Christmas gift was one of the hardest things I had done so far in my grieving process. It was so personal to my husband and so final for me.

The notes needed to say just how important this gift was, but I struggled to find the right words. No matter what I wrote, it didn't convey how important this was to him. I finally had to let go and just prepare the gift for each recipient. I couldn't control what it meant to them. Worrying was pointless.

61

The First New Year's Eve

"I don't like bad feelings gnawing away at me".
~ Sarah McLachlan

I planned a party for New Year's Eve and invited a group of friends to spend time with me. They all graciously accepted. The menu was planned, the party hats and horns placed on the table, and the playing cards were out. I had been looking forward to New Year's Eve, the party, the food, and the company. But spending that first New Year's Eve without my husband was excruciating. I thought by then, the horrible memories of hospital stays and procedures, his death, and subsequent funeral would come to an end. I convinced myself that all I had to do was make it through New Year's Eve, and next year would be different.

My friends were wonderful, and the game of cards was invigorating. The food was only fair as I managed to burn the beef tenderloin to a crisp. As the clock ticked away, I became more uncomfortable. The closer to midnight, the greater was my sense of loss and dread. It became overpowering. My plan to distract myself through the evening was failing.

As the clock struck 12:00, the hugs and the kisses commenced, but my heart was aching. By 12:01, I knew that nothing had changed. I got a glimpse of the depth of my denial. I felt foolish and vulnerable for believing that getting from New Year's Eve to New Year's day would make a difference.

62

The Trust in Self

"Trust your own instincts, go inside, follow your heart. Right from the start. Go ahead and stand up for what you believe in. As I've learned, that's the path to happiness."
~ Lesley Ann Warren

In the past, New Year's Day would have been packed with things that I planned to do differently. Those momentary heartfelt resolutions ranged from exercising more, eating healthier, the new whatever diet, and stopping spending extra money. I had looked at this date as a beginning, a starting point for a positive resolution that was usually driven by want or a need to change something, which in the end never lasted.

But this New Year's Day was different as it was the first one in twenty years without my loved one. I was determined to focus on something positive, trust myself and make a decision that would make this resolution different from the empty promises that typically happened on this day.

So, what would I change that would make a difference? I took a look at my life and knew I was drowning in sadness; the scary part was that I didn't know how I could change this. So instead of making a long-term resolution, I decided to focus on what seemed

129

like the next right thing. The next right thing was to make a plan, and maybe by doing this, I would get some relief. Or I could make a decision to do nothing and continue to feel the same.

So, on New Year's Day, I sat down with a pen and focused on putting a plan together to relieve my sadness. My plan included continuing to participate in my support group, finding one positive thing within each day, and finding a way to share my experience to help others. I also needed to remember that my husband had really died.

I knew there were no guarantees with any plan that I put together; however, this was the path that I chose with the hope of decreasing my sadness. Doing the next right thing I believed I could continue to heal.

63

The Snow Day

"I live about 60 miles northwest of New York City, and whenever there's news of a big snowstorm coming, everyone runs for the store. The perishable items are usually the first things to go, which doesn't make sense because they perish."
~ *Susan Beth Pfeffer*

For several days the weather report predicted a major snowstorm in my area. I went to the store and got my storm essentials: batteries for flashlights, gas for the generator, salt for the driveway, bottled water, and canned foods. I dragged a ¼ cord of wood into my garage and got something sweet to eat.

In the past, an impending snowstorm caused anxiety. Due to my loved one's illness, the preparations were extensive. We had to be sure there were plenty of oxygen tanks, the prescriptions were all filled, and be prepared to keep the driveway as clean as possible in case we had to call for an ambulance.

But today was different. This was the first major snowstorm I would be going through on my own. I found myself enjoying the thought of a real snow day. We had lived in the northeast for twelve years, and this snow day would be my first with no worries. It reminded me of the kind of snow day that the kids look forward to – simply fun, relaxing, book reading, game playing, and eating comfort food.

I put together a pot of soup. It simmered on the stove. The fireplace had warmed the living room, and I sat on the bench in front of my picture window, enjoying the view as the snow started to fall. The flakes were big and beautiful, and it didn't take long for the woods to be blanketed by snow.

This was the perfect snow day. I was filled with gratitude and appreciation for the beautiful woods around my home. Even though there would be three feet of snow in the morning, I enjoyed the quiet that came with this storm. I sat on my couch and realized that the snowy peace was actually calming my soul.

64

The Alone Factor

"Every night when I go to bed, I hope that I may never wake again, and every morning renews my grief."
~ Franz Schubert

Having committed to participate in grief therapy, I found myself speaking of feelings that I didn't know I had. Although I wasn't actively suicidal, I had decided that it would be okay if I passed. The grief had taken hold of me and was sucking the life out of me. Thankfully, I brought this awareness to therapy, which helped me explore these changes.

I no longer recognized my life. The most significant change was what I called "the alone factor." Waking up. Eating. Cooking. Watching television. Driving. Sitting in front of the fireplace. And sleeping. Alone.

This realization touched my core and consumed me with sadness.

Everything in my life was built around being alone, and I wasn't sure how to move forward. My friends would invite me to spend time with them; however, there was always the race to return home so I could be alone. It seemed to be the only way that I felt comfortable and safe. Working with my therapist, I shared that I needed to find a way to bring purpose back into my life. We discussed my attending a grief group, exploring potential hobbies, and eventually returning to work.

I called a close friend to discuss these options. She reminded me of how important it was to find joy and meaning. It didn't matter if it was painting, music, volunteering, or work – all that mattered was that people needed to find something to fill their hearts.

With this thought in mind I picked up the phone and made arrangements to return to work. I needed to feel productive and, even though I knew I was still distracted, it was a place to begin. Returning to work reminded me that life really does go on – even in the face of a devastating loss. Perhaps this could be the beginning of bringing me back to life. I was willing to trust that my steps had been guided back onto the right path – simply by picking up the phone.

65

The Return to Work

"Being productive at your craft is important. Being productive in your devotion to grow as a human is essential."
~ Robin S. Sharma

Even though I was afraid of how others would view me, I returned to work after seventy-nine days and a bit of therapy. I returned to a bit of normalcy from my former life. Upon my return, co-workers and friends shared their condolences, and my work life began again.

I had a hard time concentrating and could not multitask. I was easily distracted, forgetful and what used to be simple now seemed overwhelming. So, in an attempt to get organized, I compiled a "to do" list. I began by doing the little things like organizing my desk and watering my plants. I started reviewing my emails and telephone calls and responded to those that demanded my attention despite my out-of-office message. But these things were completed within a couple of days, leaving me in my cubicle in despair. I needed a project that would allow me to get lost in my work.

I began reviewing my upcoming class schedule to see what needed to be done. I picked a class that needed a lot of work. I began the updating process by researching what had changed, developing the new class materials, and then designing the student workshops to keep everyone engaged, including myself. This was the perfect activity as I found myself getting lost in the minutia without the distraction of my grief.

Despite my initial fear of letting others see my grief after returning to work, I found myself grateful. I kept busy by revamping the outdated materials. I felt valuable and productive and my days seemed to fly by. As I think back to those early months, I am in complete awe that I survived by just putting one foot in front of the other. The real benefit was allowing my grief to become a part of my life instead of taking over completely.

66

The Co-workers

"God has blessed me with an amazing family, friends, and work
colleagues that have been my joy, my support, and my sanity.
I don't know what I'd do without them."
~ Josie Loren

I have been blessed to have a wonderful group of people at my employment. They have been creative, intelligent, motivated, shared their ideas, and embraced mine. And there are a special few who showed up and became part of our life when it was tough and not pretty. They became friends.

They showed up to my loved one's art openings through the years. They came to the hospital to keep me company when he was in ICU. They took my calls during the day when I was consumed with the overwhelming fear that he would die. They came to his wake and funeral and let me cry when I needed to. They called when I took a six-week leave of absence from my job and came to help with moving furniture, stacking wood, and blowing away the autumn leaves.

I returned to work, and I tried not to cry. But, when I did, my co-workers supported me. When I thought they were sick of me and my grief, they said the things to let me know it was fine. The invitations to dinner, movies, and shared holidays, their kind words, and cards consistently showed me their friendship.

Returning to work was a lot harder than I thought it would be. I was distracted, depressed, angry, impatient, and forgetful. My coworkers continued to listen when I needed to talk, they let me cry when I was going through my grief-quakes, and on occasion, they even joined me.

I am beyond grateful. The kindness of these individuals prevented me from losing my mind and working helped me re-establish a routine and a purpose. I continued to have faith that my coworkers would be there for me, and I am overwhelmed with appreciation for them.

67

The How Are You Feeling?

*"Expressing my feelings and then the opportunity to
share with others is just such a gift."
~ Mattie Stepanek*

After my loved one's death, people would ask how I was feeling, and I would attempt to just answer with "I'm fine." "I'm fine" was saved for acquaintances and people I would see in the hallways at work, people who really didn't need to know. There was also a group of people who were so uncomfortable that they didn't want to know.

However, when asked by close friends, my responses were different. Deep down, I knew they understood the healing that happens when we share truthfully with each other. I have learned that sharing painful moments is the beginning of letting go of my grief. It was easier to answer when close friends asked how I was feeling. The flood gates would open. Feeling safe, I would tell them how awful it was to lose a spouse. I am forever in their debt for allowing me to share my truth even though it was filled with painful memories.

It had only been a few months since his passing, and there was no way that my life was coming together. Those who knew me understood that. Those in the know included my children and grandchildren. It was difficult to answer them when they asked how I was doing; they also missed their loved one and were experiencing their own grief. I am forever grateful for the love and support of my children, who allow me to just be wherever I am.

68

Welcome to the Thanatologist Corner

"My prayer is to learn new things, imbibe fresh insights. You must not take life too seriously. You must enjoy the process of living."
~ Sonu Nigam

Life has allowed me to cross paths with some fabulous people and connect with some of them for the long haul. One of these is the woman who hired me when my son was an infant, more than thirty years ago. This began one of my longest-lasting friendships, a long history that created an unbreakable bond. She has witnessed my failings, supported me through life's tragedies, loved me through my endeavors, and during my time of grief. Her support has never faltered.

After my loved one passed, she called and visited often. She knew I was struggling, and having worked at a hospice facility for many years, she put together a letter that included an article from 'The Thanatologist Corner.' The first thing I did was to look up what thanatology was. The dictionary noted it was the "study of the effects of death and dying, especially the investigation of ways to lessen the suffering and the needs of the terminally ill and their survivors."

141

While reading the article, it occurred to me that it contained basic, common-sense information and simple suggestions. I was in no state of mind to even notice that I wasn't practicing those things. Since my husband's death, I had criticized myself for not being strong enough and thinking of my forgetfulness as an impairment. Of course I was stuffing my feelings. I found them inappropriate. Unacceptable.

Since the article had come from such a trusted source, I read it again. Simple, common-sense suggestions.

I began to pay attention to how I treated myself. The key was to take a moment and just allow myself to be where I was – minus the endless criticism. On the days I mistreat myself, I ask a higher power for patience and forgiveness. On the days that I am aware and able to notice, I work as diligently on loving myself the way my friend loves me.

69

The Convention

"When you're surrounded by all these people, it can be even lonelier than when you're by yourself. You can be in a huge crowd, but if you don't feel like you can trust anybody or talk to anybody, you feel like you're really alone."
~ *Fiona Apple*

Every year I would look forward to attending a convention focused on spiritual enrichment, meditation, and serving others.

I'd purchase my registration as soon as I could because the convention was always something special to look forward to. In the past, I would get excited in anticipation of attending the workshops and hearing the speakers with their encouraging messages. Other friends came from a distance. I didn't often see them, so the opportunity to socialize together was always an added bonus. Finally, the entire experience provided me with a sense of connection which reinforced why I continued to attend.

This particular year I was on my way to the convention anticipating the joy and excitement I'd felt in the past. As I drove closer to the event, I started feeling an emptiness – a void that attending could not fill. I found myself praying for the courage to merely show up and do my best.

As I walked into the hotel, I started seeing others in the lobby with that look of excitement. After checking into my room, I stood in line for convention registration, surrounded by people projecting what this weekend would be like. Initially, I thought that showing up would make me feel a part of the crowd, that I'd be able to connect to that excitement. However, like everything else in my life, this was different.

I realized my head was doing its best to short-change my experience. I had just walked into the convention, hadn't attended one single workshop, and wanted to leave. Even though this was not like the previous years, I had faith that I would still benefit by participating. I said a quick prayer and committed to myself to focus on doing the next right thing.

Only eighty days had passed since my loved one's death, yet I chose to focus on my gratitude. I was reminded that the excitement, connection, and unity that I'd felt at past conventions had only happened when I showed up and participated. So, setting foot into my first workshop, I knew this simple act would allow me to begin enjoying this weekend.

70

The Halls

"A work of art is a world in itself reflecting senses
and emotions of the artist's world."
~ Hans Hofmann

One of my oldest friends came to visit and support me as I acclimated to life as a widow. It was fantastic to see her come down my driveway. The moment she stepped onto the porch, we hugged. And we cried. We spent a few days together talking, which really means I shed additional tears as she listened and held me. We were able to take walks and explore my neighborhood, do a little hiking, go out to dinner, and a long-time favorite activity: a visit to my local museum.

From my earliest childhood, I have been drawn to the arts. One of my favorite memories is of a school field trip where we saw one of the most extensive exhibits of Van Gogh paintings to travel in the United States. I remember walking through the halls in awe of these fabulous, colorful, and unique paintings. It made a huge impact and, for the rest of my life, impressionist paintings remained one of my favorite styles.

So it was no surprise that I fell in love with an artist and shared a passion for art and, more specifically, paintings throughout our marriage. Sure, he liked Warhol, and I was into Van Gogh. Still, we enjoyed going to art museums and simply walking around to appreciate the diverse exhibits. Wherever we lived, we would frequent museums and explore their collections. Sadly, walking around museum halls became such a challenge that we eventually had to stop going.

When I got to our local museum with my friend, I tried to block out the last time I was there. It had been more than a year, but the image of my husband struggling to walk was etched into my thoughts. Despite those memories, I wanted to let go and enjoy this experience.

As my friend and I stepped foot into the main gallery, I was relieved to find that I could share the love of a museum with someone who is not my husband. I felt grateful that we were two friends talking, wandering the halls, and enjoying the museum.

71

The Anger

"Anybody can become angry – that is easy, but to be angry with the right person and to the right degree and at the right time and for the right purpose, and in the right way – that is not within everybody's power and is not easy."
~ Aristotle

Anger had found me, and I did not know what to do with it. I was angry all the time. I had a right to be angry. Illness had taken my loved one, and I was without my partner. All was not right with the world. My life had changed, and I was pissed off.

I walked through these days as if it was OK to take out my wrath on inconsiderate drivers, slow store clerks, or the person on the other end of the phone. I would try to keep myself together, but all I had to do was get in the car. At the first mistake by the ass driving next to me, I would rise to an anger level much too large for the situation. I never got mad at the right person. So, who was the right person?

It took me a while to realize that I was angry at him. And me. I was pissed off that he did not take care of himself through the years, that we did not do more while he was well, that we did not have more time together. But I was furious that he lived through that horrible surgery only to die fourteen days later. I was freakin' angry that he died and left me alone.

I knew it was not OK to live this way; the anger I was expressing was leaving a path of destruction from which I would not be able to recover. I had no purpose, no direction, and no clue what to do next. Something had to change.

So, I picked up the phone and spoke with a wise friend. She suggested that I write a letter to him about my anger and disappointments. Once I had written this letter, I made my way to the cemetery. I reached the grave, full of apprehension, but read him my letter. I sobbed as I said things that I had hidden in my heart. I felt a little lighter when I left the cemetery. I did not know if it was due to the letter or the tears and emotions at his gravesite. It probably doesn't matter.

At fifty-six days since my loved one passed, and I'm still angry. I am making my way back to a better place as I recognize that anger is undoubtedly part of the grief process, one I am trying desperately to navigate.

72

The Writing and the Choices

*"It's pretty cathartic for me to write a letter to God
and tell him what I'm praying for that day or what
I'm going through emotionally."*
~ Ainsley Earhardt

As the days passed, I realized that I had been feeling angrier
and angrier and was unclear what was bringing these feelings to
the surface. From my experience, I knew that when confronted
with situations that seemed overwhelming, all I needed to do was
to pick up a pen to discover what was really going on with me. I sat
on my couch and began to write a letter addressing all the things
that I was angry about. To my amazement, it did not take a long
time to complete.

I was angry over the constant medical care, the fear and dread
that was always beneath the surface, my loved one's inability to
care for himself or to be there for me, for all the medicines, special
foods, bathing, cleaning, and my working to take care of us.

But as I wrote, realization shifted from my anger with him to
my awareness of how angry I was with myself. I was angry that I
had attempted to manage and control an unmanageable situation.
I was angry that I was alone, feeling insignificant and uncared for.

I was disappointed and heartbroken with the people in my life. The worst thing was that although I had previously addressed my anger, it had grown to encompass my job, our children, the last hospital stay, and my loved one.

As I continued to write, self-pity took over, and the shame stepped in. I was ashamed of what I was feeling. Because of the shame, I had kept it secret from everyone. How could I be angry with someone who had been sick for years and now was dead? How could I have resentment toward my loved one for being sick? Looking at this made me feel small, self-centered, and ugly.

I had written for an hour and now had some choices to make. As prayer had worked in the past, I began to pray for healing from the years of being in fear, of the constant uncertainty, and finally for the anger to be removed as it was always beneath the surface. I asked for acceptance for my resentments and for being where I was. I hoped to get a reprieve from my angry feelings. I wanted to start focusing on the other part of our lives where the love and the good we shared still existed. When I was done with my prayers, I felt calmer, and ended my day with gratitude and faith. A higher power took care of me for one more day.

73

The Impact

"There's no greater gift than thinking that you had some impact on the world, for the better."
~ Gloria Steinem

Every once in a while, I find myself going back to the handful of days following my loved one's death. I log into my Facebook account to re-read what people posted about him and, on occasion, find something new. I knew that he had deeply touched my life. From the types of movies that became part of my repertoire to the art and artists that influenced him and now provided me with a more textured world – his fingerprints are everywhere. Even music was different. Better. It was something we both had a passion for. The differences in our sensibilities enabled us to share what we each loved and broadened our appreciation.

But he had also impacted more people than I ever imagined. Being an artist and on the board of directors at an artists co-op, he had developed friends who followed his website and art shows. Despite ending his career prematurely, he maintained friendships with a group of elite runners. We were blessed with a group of loyal friends. After his death, several of them changed their social media profile pictures to the black and white photographs he had taken of them. Others changed theirs to one of his paintings. Then there were the multiple posts about him. There was something special about seeing his paintings, their comments, and short tributes throughout my Facebook feed. The loving tributes were from others' perspectives and not just mine.

Today I find myself very aware of his impact on my life and the lives of others. I wonder why I care. I have come to believe that it makes me feel less alone to have other people see him as I did: kind-hearted, passionate, caring, and grateful for every moment he had. Despite being paralyzed with loss, I miss him terribly. The Facebook posts reinforce my memories of his sense of humor, work ethic, and talent that made all our lives richer and definitely more colorful.

74

The Lens

"We don't see things as they are, we see them as we are."
~ Anais Nin

As a member of the human race, I experience life through the lens I was born with. I struggled with my lens for many years and I began seeing patterns I didn't like. I would wake up, and my first conscious realization was that I was broken and damaged. I was drowning in grief and self-pity. First I judged myself and then questioned if this was what I was supposed to feel like.

The people in my life treated me with a mixture of gentleness and apprehension to avoid causing additional stress. Of course, this cascaded into increased feelings of vulnerability and discomfort. So, I'd put on a stiff upper lip and remind everyone that I was just fine. I encouraged my friends to reach out with their struggles and let them know that it was helpful when they did. It saved me from focusing on myself.

Sometimes it's hard to be grateful for ugly life events and questionable choices, but those are what helped me make many adjustments. My lens was changing from selfish and self-centered to grateful and humble. I'm convinced that changes in my lens allowed me to see, fall in love and create a life with my partner. But, falling in love doesn't prevent life from happening. We struggled with continued health challenges, which eventually led to my loved one's death.

While the change in my lens occurred rather quickly, this changed perspective required me to go back to basics. I needed to be sure that I was eating regularly and getting enough sleep, to participate in my support group and share how I felt.

Still, when the house is quiet and my mind wanders, the image that haunts me is of my loved one's last breath. It won't go away. So, I allow my memory to fill in the blanks and the image of him opening his eyes and taking his last breath fills the deepest part of my soul. Two of our children, a close friend, and I were with him when he made his transition.

Until that time he suffered more than anyone should, and just being there with him has provided more than enough painful memories for a lifetime.

Today, I remind myself that to move from a bad mental space all I needed to change was my perspective. I have come to know that things in my life can change in a heartbeat, and what I choose to do with that change will make the difference. As long as I practice gratitude, my lens will be clear and show me a the path.

Today I have a choice about the way I view the memory of the children arriving at his death bed, and all of us surrounding him in the intensive care unit. I was standing on one side of his bed when my friend said he had opened his eyes. I quickly glanced at him, he closed his eyes and took his last breath. I knew instantly that his suffering was over and that mine was to begin.

But today I chose to add this final thought to this memory. The last breath was a culmination of twenty years of illness and a life filled with physical and emotional pain. But as painful as it was to watch, I know what a privilege it is to be there for someone you love. I am indebted to my children and my friend for being there. I am grateful he was surrounded by the love of family and not by strangers or, worse, alone. That truly was a blessing.

As time passed, I learned better coping skills, incorporating them into my day-to-day actions. Through this evolution, I began to see what my life offered.

Well-meaning friends suggested I focus on the positive but seeing life through the perception of grief made that nearly impossible. Everything I looked at was colored by grief, my distorted view that things would never get better, or I'd never again get a whole night's sleep.

Whatever we focus on grows, so I knew that continuing to focus on how broken or damaged I felt, wouldn't allow me to see the healing or growth that had already taken place. So, I committed to getting some help to focus on the positive and keep my automatic reaction in check. The most significant adjustment came from participating in an email gratitude list with a group of women friends.

As easy as it would have been to interpret every bump in the road as the end of the world, I saw how things really were: I had a great job, a family I love, and beautiful friends who love me. That's a lot to be grateful for, and that gratitude would carry me through another day.

Hope springs from having gratitude, and it will find a way back into my life.

75

The Last Task

*"Keep every promise you make and
only make promises you can keep."*
~ *Anthony Hitt*

After twenty years of marriage, things had been briefly mentioned that stick with me still. The thoughts range from insignificant chatter to final requests. None of those requests were formally written into a will: he trusted that I would remember and follow through with making his wishes come true.

As overwhelmed and grief-stricken as I was, a memory pops into my head of my loved one's determination to get things done. Months before his passing, he seemed to hit a new level of realization regarding his ill health and impending death. This drove him to ensure his legacy – his artwork – was in good shape. He made a list of everything that had to be done and tackled the various items on the list one by one.

He diligently worked on his website to confirm it was up-to-date with all his paintings, photography, and poetry. Then he developed a plan on how to proceed with the paintings. Despite being quite ill, he asked some friends to help organize his studio. That meant that every oil painting was taken out of the bins to be reviewed and inspected. Then they carefully removed huge digital art canvases to a flat surface for review, inspection, and, if necessary, signing.

The three of them were in the studio for hours. At the end of these sessions, he was beyond exhausted. He was also happy to have accomplished the next task on the list. After he rested, he wanted to talk about the last task, knowing that this one could only be performed after his death. Knowing that our son had the skills to do so, he asked that I keep his website up and running for two years to display his art, poetry, and photography.

Three months after my beloved passed, I ventured to his website to ensure that the last task had been accomplished. As I clicked on the link, I was immediately at his site, and I found myself in tears. It is beautiful, and I was flooded with memories of him working and creating. I was overwhelmed with how much I miss him but struck by the trust that my husband had, knowing that I would do whatever I could to fulfill the promise of this last task. I reached for the tissue box, and was grateful for our son.

76

The Punishing God

*"I no longer believe that I'm going to be struck
down by a punishing God."*
~ Bari Weiss

As a young adult, my concept of God was always shrouded in the most negative of traits. God was stern, harsh, unforgiving, vengeful, and worst of all – punishing. However, through the years, I reassessed the characteristics of a god that I wanted to have in my life. Once I became willing to consider another type of god, I heard people share that they had a forgiving, compassionate, understanding, kind and loving god. As people shared about their experiences with faith, I was able to borrow some of those positive traits and eventually find an image that worked for me.

However, after my loved one's death, I heard someone talk about god answering their prayers – that their loved one had been spared. I began to doubt my god. I couldn't shake the thought that God must not have been listening to my prayers. I questioned how a kind and loving god could let someone suffer, and, for a moment, I slipped back to my old concept of the punishing god. I was stuck on the last three weeks of my loved one's life and how no one should have to suffer like that.

I began to ask those philosophical questions everyone eventually asks while determining their correct spiritual path. Does it include a god, no god, or does the path lead them to agnosticism? For myself, I came to believe that my god wouldn't let someone die, and my god wouldn't save anyone either. My faith was that I would be given the strength to deal with the outcome, whatever happened. I began to look at the life I shared with my loved one. What I saw were years of ambulance rides, physician visits, specialists, and countless hospitalizations. I shifted my focus to the positive. He had come to the brink of death many times and had gotten through to the other side. The god I had grown to know and trust hadn't given up on us: it was simply my loved one's time.

Sitting with my thoughts, I find myself remembering all the gifts received through the years and can trust this comforting god again. I am grateful my life crossed paths with this remarkable man. I shared a life that was unexpected, colorful, and filled with beauty to balance the heartache that real life brings to everyone.

77

The Visit

"We will all, someday, experience death, and become obsolete
as a dead leaf falling from a tree, crushed by passersby
to ashes underlying the earth."
~ Kim Elizabeth

My whole life, I had been uncomfortable with anything related
to death. I wanted to avoid visiting my husband's grave. If I avoided his grave long enough, somehow, his death wouldn't be real. But
avoiding those visits compounded my grief – I could add guilt and
shame for not going sooner. How could a loving wife not go to the
cemetery to visit her husband's grave?

I made a plan to go to the cemetery. I had only been there once
– for the funeral – so I relied on my GPS to find the most direct
way. The guilt and shame did not get me to go one minute sooner
than I was supposed to. But I needed to get there and walk through
the uncomfortable feelings.

Once there, I struggled to find his grave. It had recently
snowed, and there was no headstone to mark it. So, I searched in
the direction of where I thought his grave would be. Out of the
corner of my eye, I spotted a small placard with his picture on
it. Walking amongst the snow-covered graves broke through my

denial: I began to sob. Despite my previous avoidance, the feelings of loss spilled out of me. It hadn't mattered that I waited three months to visit: he was still dead. Whatever denial I had was gone.

It had only been ninety-one days since my loved one passed, and I survived this first visit to his grave. Yes, there were many tears, but it was essential to acknowledge that I had survived. Somehow, I thought I was not strong enough to endure this kind of pain. I found the courage to sit by his grave by deciding to go. The tears shed began to wash away some of my grief. That first visit taught me that I could walk through my fear. I now knew that I would be able to visit the grave again.

78

The Pause, Prayer, and Reset

"You can always cope with the present moment, but you cannot cope with something that is only a mind projection – you cannot cope with the future."
~ Eckhart Tolle

I had made plans to meet a friend for dinner and a play but was very apprehensive. Tonight was the third production of the season and the first I would attend without him. My thoughts betrayed me and wandered to what these tickets actually represented: the nightmare of the only one he gots to see and the others he would never get to enjoy.

Even though the upcoming evening was starting off rocky, I knew I could turn these feelings around. I paused, said a quick prayer, and started my day over. Nobody ever said that a day had to begin when we first got out of bed and starting my day over always worked. It's an attitude reset, an opportunity to begin again. It didn't matter what had taken place during the previous eight hours — only what I was going to do right now. I made an effort to dress for the occasion.

When I arrived at the restaurant and saw her, my apprehension faded. I can't tell you what we spoke about, but I know that I started to enjoy the evening out. I felt some anxiety walking into the theater, but my people-watching habit quickly took it away. We made our way to our seats, and I noticed that the play was a musical. As the curtain rose and the music began, I remembered that she was sitting in my husband's seat. When the uncomfortable feelings started, I again paused, prayed, and reset my thoughts. I was able to permit myself to be immersed in everything good about being at a live show.

It had been three months since my loved one passed, and I was sitting in the front row of a musical, seeing and hearing the actors. To my surprise, I found that I enjoyed being there. Resetting my attitude allowed me to let go of my apprehensions, be grateful, and enjoy this moment.

79

The Garden Magazines

"Remember that children, marriages, and flower gardens
reflect the kind of care they get."
~ H. Jackson Brown, Jr.

Winter was the time of year for looking at garden magazines
and catalogs. I have always enjoyed letting my mind envision how
my garden would look in the upcoming spring, summer, and fall.
I would look forward to inspecting the land, physically drawing a
map, and planning what areas of the garden needed to be trans-
planted, removed, or trimmed back. Even during the wildest of
winter storms, reviewing my gardening magazines always provided
hope that spring and the beautiful flowers were coming.

I reviewed magazines, books, and websites, carefully reading
the descriptions. This helped me determine which plants were appropriate for my zone, what necessary temperatures, which plants
were deer resistant, and, finally, their delivery date. To thrive, they
had to be planted at just the right time.

The pile of garden magazines on my dining room table did not
interest me. The previously joyful winter pastime now made me
even more aware that I was stuck in a dark place. The disconnect
between «then» and «now» simply added to my sadness. I couldn›t

even remember the beauty that my perennials brought every year, and worse, I was somehow denying the joy that I felt when they came.

I knew that I had to become more grounded because what I was feeling wasn't the whole truth. The truth was that for that day, and only that day, I was unwilling to look at the pictures and dream of my garden. I promptly stopped my thoughts and asked my higher power for a moment of clarity. I remembered that in past years this was the time that would give me feelings of hope, resurgence, and joy in anticipation of the beauty that was coming.

On that day, what I wanted was to sit in front of a fire, wrapping my body and mind in a warm blanket. And there was a new truth: even though I wasn't willing to review and plan my garden that day, I had a bit of hope that perhaps tomorrow I would.

80

The Action

"Action expresses priorities."
~ Mahatma Gandhi

After my loved one's death, I was stuck in a place where the emptiness left me capable of performing only routine tasks. I pretended to be functioning in most areas of my life while earning a living. However, I knew I wasn't okay, and so did my close network.

If I was to heal, I needed to do something different, and that would involve taking action. The problem was that I wasn't sure what that action should be. I was connecting with my support system, had a full-time job that helped me feel productive, and saw a professional to deal with my grief. But I was still stuck.

With pen and paper in hand, I decided to write about my options and what action I could take to let go of the judgment and my lack of self-acceptance. Clearly, I was judging myself for having feelings and for not doing as well as I thought a widow should.

It became apparent that the culprit was twofold: I was impatient with what I should be feeling, and worse, my expectations continued to be that I should be doing better. One of my earliest lessons as an adult came to mind where I identified how negative the word SHOULD is for me. To this day, anytime I use the word should I know that my expectation of others, especially myself, will be full of judgment, self-defeating, and lacking compassion. And I was getting very tired of adding self-inflicted wounds to my already painful bereavement.

I sat on my bench overlooking the woods, took a deep cleansing breath, and began to meditate on my new intention to let go of the 'shoulds' and my harsh expectations – especially the ones I had for myself. So I made a conscious decision to put a new priority in motion that would enable me to take action and let go of my brutal judgment.

At first, I struggled. Thoughts invaded my consciousness, but meditation takes practice as with any new skill. My commitment remains to take that quiet time to sit and breathe. Doing this has enabled me to focus on being present and letting that be good enough.

81

The Moment

"Doing the best at this moment puts you in
the best place for the next moment."
~ Oprah Winfrey

Often, taking a breath in the now keeps me focused on my
life. I was surprised to eventually awaken one morning feeling
spiritually centered. Nothing could touch me. But as the moment
stretched into an hour, I sank into my reality. At that moment, I
was sad, and I was lost. The pain was unbearable, and all hope had
been sucked out of the atmosphere.

But there is more than the pain of life. I also feel love for
my children and grandchildren, and I am reminded that I have
a life that›s worth having. I remember that no matter what has
happened, I am safe, and I have people who love and care for me.
My friends remind me of the importance of staying in the moment
and that staying there is a gift we get by living this life.

When I find myself slipping and wandering into my past, the
pain reminds me that my loved one is gone. Whatever that life may
have been, staying in that moment is torturous. When I step into
the future, I am acutely aware that my loved one is not there either.
He can no longer comfort me, keep me company or share in my

current life. I find that the only place to live is in this moment, and if I step out of it, everything seems worse.

Now that my loved one has passed, I am reminded that this moment is where I need to be, no matter what direction life has taken me. At this moment, I can speak to a couple of very close friends and remember that despite the distance, they have been available, any time of day or night. At this moment, I see my friends deal with life on life's terms. I can keep my faith in this moment, knowing that I have always been taken care of. For a moment, my heart knows I am exactly where I am supposed to be.

82

The Past Happy

"If you win all the time, you lose the drama in life. To make the happy moments happy, you need the sad moments too."
~ Doug Davidson

I make it a point to look at the glass as half full vs. half empty. However, since the death of my loved one, I had been unable to see good in the life we shared for twenty years.

Most of the time, I just seemed to be fighting back the grief. When I tried to focus on our happy moments, only the years of hospitals and illness came to mind. I knew there had been many moments of happiness, so I began a mission: I started listing some of the happiest things and events we shared. As I remembered a happy moment, I would pull out my notebook and jot it down. At first, I could only connect with a few, but more memories surfaced as time passed. So, the list began:

- How we laughed the night we came home from our wedding.
- How he would protest about wearing the Santa hat…but how much he came to enjoy Christmas mornings.
- Making love.

- Him lying on a hammock at my parents' farm.
- How he wrapped his legs into a pretzel as the kids and I made fun of him.
- How he listened to the women around our dining room table talk about men and just shake his head.
- Our ninth wedding anniversary dinner in Hawaii.
- Dancing to Spanish music in Florida.
- Watching him take pictures of the ground as he searched for textures.

Finding good memories to balance the sad ones is an ongoing process. It has taken time, but the list continues to grow. I am incredibly grateful to have recovered these moments. They remind me that, despite years of illness, there were many moments of joy and happiness. They confirm that we shared a good life.

83

The Joy of Cooking

"I just really love having dinner parties and hanging out."
~ Lauren Ambrose

I used to think how odd it was that so many of our memories were centered around cooking and sitting around our dining room table. In retrospect, it makes absolute sense. Those memories were part of a beautiful experience, opening our home to family and friends to celebrate an anniversary or have a Saturday night card game. I have lots of memories of love shared, abundant laughter and hours spent around the kitchen island cooking and talking. The table was always decorated for the occasion and usually loaded with food for everyone to enjoy. Creating a warm and caring home was our goal throughout our marriage, and it was one of our most significant accomplishments.

The last year of my loved one's life was different. Once he became homebound, emotional support was more difficult to access. I didn't feel that his illness should deprive him of the joy that friends brought so I made an effort to maintain a social life. His immune deficiency meant we could only have a few people at the house so I extended a handful of invitations to sit around our dining room table eating, playing cards, conversing, and enjoying whatever laughter we could muster. It was an attempt to provide him with a love-filled social life and forget his illness for a while.

Yet the joy we had experienced around the dining room table was becoming a memory. His compromised immune system and lack of appetite made everything more complicated. It was gratifying to simply provide a meal that he could enjoy.

I'm one of those people who took cooking in stride. I can't say I cooked every day, but I cooked enough to enjoy what I made. As the years passed and my life changed, I found a lot of joy cooking for my new blended family and our friends who were like family.

I thought that after he died I would again find pleasure in creating meals. However, after his passing, the concept of entertaining didn't feel appropriate or natural. It was uncomfortable to think about bringing people into what used to be our home. I discovered the connection to joy was not simply cooking. That delight came from cooking for others.

Having no experience with this new life left me a blank slate. At the urging of my mentor, I began by putting together a list of things I wanted to do. I remembered how much happiness I had gotten out of having people come to the house and preparing dinner for them. I felt the nervous energy when I was getting the house in order, the joy I felt while preparing the food, and the love I shared as our guests walked into the house. I wanted and needed to experience this again.

So, today I give myself permission to start doing some of the things I love to do. Entertaining was at the top of my list. I decided to make a guest list for a small dinner party, and I immediately knew it would bring me joy. Just by thinking of planning the dinner party, I found myself smiling.

84

The Difference

*"If you want to have a good sleep, you have
to have a good mattress."*
~ Jonathan Scott

My loved one's illness brought us to the living room for the last three years of his life – him in his recliner and me on my chaise. Several weeks after his death, I continued to sleep in the living room and, of course, judged myself harshly for that. Something needed to change before I could move back into our bedroom.

After his closet was emptied, some furniture sold, and everything removed from the walls, my oldest friend came to visit with one task in mind – to paint my bedroom. The journey began with picking just the right colors for the walls, and after several trips to the hardware store, we left with two gallons of paint. My friend did a beautiful job, and the room felt lighter. I thought this would make the difference.

Now came the crown molding and baseboards. A contractor friend put in the lovely molding because I thought this would make the difference. I went on a mission to buy a new comfortable mattress as the one I had was lumpy with memories of illness and death. Somehow a new mattress would make the difference.

Finally, multiple trips to Pottery Barn added the finishing touches of linens, drapes, and comforters to complete the room. It was now beautiful, light, warm, and filled with my loved one's artwork because this would make the difference.

The room was lovely, but the memories of illness were still there, so I continued to sleep on the living room chaise. None of those changes to the bedroom brought about the difference I sought. The chaise is where I felt the strongest connection to him, so I decided to give myself whatever amount of time I needed. Eventually, I would move upstairs to my lovely bedroom because, when it happens, it will have made a difference.

85

The Camera

"Holding on to things from the past is the same as clinging to an image of yourself in the past. If you're the least bit interested in changing anything about yourself, I suggest you be brave and start letting things go."
~ Fumio Sasaki

When my loved one and I were married, he kept extremely busy. When he worked, he was a great web designer, but after the illness took hold of his life, he focused solely on his creative endeavors: painting, writing, and photography, displaying his enormous talent.

One of his favorite creative outlets was photography. He would take closeups of everyday objects in the endless search for different textures. He worked hard to stay relevant and on top of all new technology so his ever-expanding repertoire would remain cutting edge.

My son came for the holidays one year, and we took a sightseeing trip to New York. We walked around the city and made our way to Strawberry Fields in Central Park. However, when I reviewed the pictures of that trip, I found that several of them had me waving my hand for him to hurry up. I remembered how irritated I was with him because he had spent endless time shooting pictures of sidewalk grates as we waited for him to catch up.

One day our daughter asked if I would be willing to let go of her father's camera. I felt protective of his camera and the memories associated with it. At that time I could not let it go as I fondly remembered the New York City sidewalk grates and the iron railing at our son's apartment in Seattle. And the wonderful picture taken in Montreal of a bright orange partial wall that remained after a building was torn down.

I felt bad that I said no, but I was not ready to let go of his camera that day. Perhaps as more time passes, it will be easier to share with the loved ones in my life but, for today, I give myself permission to keep and cherish it for myself.

86

The First, the Second, the Third Valentine's Day

"When you give a homemade gift, you are giving a part of yourself to the recipient. You can't do that with a mass-produced item."
~ Mark Frauenfelder

I had been miserable and suffering in anticipation of the first Valentine's Day without him. For a least two weeks leading to this made-up holiday, I felt uneasy, and when the day arrived, I felt low, unloved, and morose.

I kept telling myself that this was not a day worth suffering over and that I would not allow myself to go there. However, knowing that this was not how I wanted to spend my day didn›t seem to matter as my thoughts kept leading me back to what I no longer had. My loved one was gone, and this day would no longer have the same meaning.

What I have learned is that I always have a choice. I can choose to look at this day filled with sadness and loss, or I can really see how blessed I was to have married an artist who left me with twenty years' worth of creative art pieces depicting his love and affection for me.

On that first Valentine's Day after my loved one's death, all I wanted was to keep that connection to my past. I wasn't ready to move forward. It had only been five months, and I was lost in the pain of self-pity as I watched commercial after commercial about what your loved one should be doing for you. Sending flowers. Buying candy. And if they really loved you, some diamond bauble. I couldn't let it go. It was not a good day.

The second Valentine's Day after his passing, I chose something different to stay connected to my feelings of love and gratitude. I went into our home office, sat by a file cabinet, and pulled out as many of his handmade cards as I could find. I opened them up with care, looked at the beautiful artwork, and with tears flowing, I reread his words.

The third Valentine's Day has come and gone. I found that I was still comforted by the cards he left me. What is clear is that I had been loved, I still feel loved, and I realized how blessed I truly am. Today this feeling will carry me through another day of my new life.

87

The Wedding Anniversary

"A wedding anniversary is the celebration of love, trust, partner-
ship, tolerance and tenacity. The order varies for any given year."
~ Paul Sweeney

Last year on this date, my husband and I went to our favorite
restaurant with six other friends to celebrate our twentieth wedding
anniversary. Due to his illness, we had an early reservation as he
couldn't be exposed to a big crowd. We ordered and received our
meals which were cooked to perfection. Everyone enjoyed desserts
and coffee. We laughed and shared delicious conversations. The
evening was as perfect as it could have been. For our twentieth
anniversary, we celebrated love, trust, and partnership.

But this year, as our wedding anniversary approached, I knew
it was supposed to be different. It was no longer our anniversary. It
had become my anniversary. And on my anniversary, I just didn't
know what I should or would be feeling. Did I need to acknowledge this day, or should I ignore the fact that we would have been
married one more year?

I decided that it was still my wedding anniversary. Although I
missed him terribly, I was still very much in love. I felt married in
my heart and in my soul. I wanted to honor that commitment and

remember what had made it so special.

For what would have been my twenty-first wedding anniversary, I made arrangements for dinner at our favorite restaurant. I celebrated this anniversary without my husband, but with the love of a friend. Despite my sadness, we shared a wonderful meal, reminisced, and shared stories about him.

After dinner, we walked over to a bookstore and wandered around talking. The bookstore had always been an after-dinner stop for my loved one and me. Tonight I shared the experience with a friend. I scoured the discounted book racks searching for some kind of art book. It then occurred that somehow, I had managed to survive the evening. All the anticipation and dread had been overcome. I ended the evening feeling love for him and the love of a friend.

88

The Headstone

"Everybody is vulnerable to being in relationships where they get fooled. I'm no different. It's just human nature."
~ Michelle Pfeiffer

One of my conversations with my loved one was about what to do with his remains. After some consideration, he said he had noticed that visiting my parents' graves seemed to bring me some peace and healing. He thought it could do the same after he was gone, so he chose to be buried.

After his death, we completed arrangements for his burial; however, it was October. One of the tasks that could not be immediately completed was to install a plaque or a headstone. I knew I'd have to wait until spring, but that would give me time to figure out the kind of marker I wanted.

Visiting the cemetery a few months after he passed, I saw how difficult it was to find his grave without a marker, so I decided to purchase a headstone. I began finding the appropriate words to pay tribute to him and made some decisions about the design; it needed to reflect his artistic sensibility.

When April came, I contacted a company to make the necessary arrangements for a lovely headstone. I paid the whole amount, and they told me it would be ready in a few months. So, in June, I contacted the vendor, was told they had made an error, that they would need to redo the headstone, and that I would get a call the moment they finished. The proprietor assured me that it would be ready for the first anniversary of his death.

I began calling weekly and sending emails in late July without receiving a response. Every time I reached out, I would get a knot in my stomach, had difficulty sleeping, and my depression would deepen. I was overwhelmed with the betrayal I felt but mustered the humility to ask a friend to help. The worst part was feeling foolish for paying all the money upfront and trusting a spiritually bankrupt company.

Almost been a year since my loved one died, and there was still no headstone. My friend got my money back, and now I would have to wait until next spring to begin this process again. We found out that the owner of the company had cheated many people. Regret and rage filled me as I realized his grave would not have a marker for at least another six months. I was in disbelief that someone could take advantage of so many grieving families. But I started my hunt for an ethical company. As soon as the weather permitted, an appropriate headstone would mark my loved one's grave.

89

The Apologies

"Accept everything about yourself – I mean everything.
You are you and that is the beginning and the end –
no apologies, no regrets."
~ Henry Kissinger

I woke up and the word 'apology' popped into my mind. I believed that it was the word of the day from my kind and loving god as I had begun to feel like I should introduce myself by saying, "My name is Rose and I'm sorry." At least once per day, I found myself crying and immediately apologizing for it. I was sure everyone had to be sick and tired of hearing my daily tale of woe, seeing the eventual tears, and listening to the apology that quickly followed.

I reacted to life in my younger years without knowing that I was not in control. So, when things happened, I would manipulate and arrange the outcome to what I believed was best for my family or myself. Doing this fed my illusion of control, and when life was hard, cruel, or sad, I stuffed my tears in an attempt to hide what I perceived as weakness. Eventually, accepting that I wasn't in control brought me feelings of vulnerability and the unexpected blessing of finding my path to tears.

I have cried from feeling disappointment, fear, and heartbreak through the years. However, shedding tears in the privacy of my home was quite a different thing than mourning in front of others. Their presence seemed to feed the vulnerability and feelings of shame, which would trigger an apology.

After what seemed like thousands of apologies for crying with friends and family, in hospitals, and at physicians' offices, I thought that the crying would finally be over once my husband died. To my surprise, it was not; it seemed that it was just getting started.

It was one hundred and thirty-eight days since my loved one died, and I'd learned two things: when overwhelmed with feelings of grief I cry, and I no longer apologize.

I understand and accept that the tears I shed are my way of letting some of my pain go. No matter what happens, I don't have to mask the pain.

90

The Seeds

"The bravest thing I ever did was continuing my life when I wanted to die."
~ Juliette Lewis

One day I woke up and realized I was lost in feelings so dark I could barely breathe. At work, I hid in my cubicle, muffling sobs, waiting for the feelings to pass. The only thing that I was sure of was that I wouldn't mind dying.

My doctor recommended that I start attending a support group where I could let some of my grief go. I tried to focus and listen to what was shared in this group, but I couldn't shake my thoughts or feelings. As hard as I tried to control these feelings, my eyes just watered, and tears rolled down my face. At the end of the meeting, I wanted to run and just get to my car before anyone approached me with comments or, worse still – questions.

I escaped the crowd and tried to identify what I was feeling. Was it desperation? Discouragement? Fear? I came to believe that the feeling was complete and utter despair. The hopelessness made me feel that I couldn't survive or cope with the intensity of this grief.

It had only been four months since my husband passed, and

I needed to give myself a break. So far I had survived the feelings of despair, anguish, and pain by simply taking some sort of action -- doing something different. Even though I saw a mental health professional and attended a group, I needed something more.

I committed to nurturing my core with meditation and prayer. There is a small stack of meditation books on my nightstand, and through prayer, I will ask for the courage and strength to continue walking through my feelings until the seeds of hope grow.

91

The First Birthday

"Many people die at twenty-five and aren›t buried
until they are seventy-five."
~ Benjamin Franklin

Ninety-nine days after my loved one passed was the day he was born. Every year, I made a big deal of the day by planning something special, often months in advance.

 Since he had been so sick for so many years, it was important to me that I commemorate this day. I would carefully consider his birthday gift, knowing that our time together was limited and that I wanted it to be remarkable. Every year had been different, and the gifts ranged from dinner at a great restaurant to a play in New York City. One year it was Montreal with tickets to Cirque de Soleil and John and Yoko's 40th Bed-In anniversary. We took a cruise to celebrate his 60th birthday.

In anticipation of the sadness this day would now bring, I made plans to meet a friend for dinner at one of my husband›s favorite restaurants. My initial thought was to go to dinner by myself. Still, instead, I reached out to a friend who had actually accompanied us for one of his birthday celebrations. She knew quite well what this day and this restaurant meant to me. She immediately said yes.

We met at the restaurant, were seated at a lovely table, ordered the fabulous food, and began to talk. The wonderful thing that came out of celebrating his birthday was that we spent the evening talking about him, especially the experiences we shared and his wicked sense of humor. I was grateful to be sharing my feelings with this particular friend.

I knew that this first birthday dinner would be painful and very difficult. But one thing that I have learned is that when I shared the pain with another person, the intensity seemed to lessen. That most certainly was my experience on that occasion. Sharing this dinner with a close friend, I was filled with hope. I knew it was OK to talk about him, miss him, and honor his birth. I am so grateful for that.

92

The Antidote

"Self-pity is our worst enemy and if we yield to it, we c an never do anything wise in this world."
~ Helen Keller

A couple of months after my loved one passed, I found my-self drowning in self-pity. Self-pity had become a very familiar emotion. All I had to do was think about the changes that life had forced upon me, and my eyes would fill with tears. Some days my thoughts wouldn't allow me to have any peace. I would ceaselessly compare myself to others, thinking about how happy they were and especially how they were not alone for Thanksgiving, Christmas, New Year's Day, or Wednesday. Along with these thoughts, the self-pity would wash over me like a warm shower.

One day was different. I wasn't venturing into the past because I was projecting into the future. I would have to deal with my loved one's birthday and our wedding anniversary in the coming weeks. I had no idea how I would survive these milestones. I was very aware that I woke up feeling depressed and couldn't wait for the day to end so I could go to bed. The self-pity I felt made it difficult to breathe or be around others. And it was beyond difficult to sit alone with my thoughts.

I knew I must humble myself and ask for help to survive these terrible feelings. The support that came to mind was to reach out and speak to my spiritual mentor. When I finally picked up the phone, she reminded me that the antidote for self-pity was gratitude, and she provided me with some suggestions. The first suggestion was to pray and meditate for peace and serenity. The second was to write a gratitude list.

Knowing that something had to change, I began praying and focusing more on gratitude. I found that just one moment of thankfulness allowed me to breathe. So, I ended the day with a pen in hand, listing everything that I was grateful for and hoping that I would be able to let the self-pity go.

93

The Drops of Coffee

*"To me, the smell of fresh-made coffee is
one of the greatest inventions."*
~ Hugh Jackman

I was sitting at a drive-through window getting ready to order my coffee when a thought crossed my mind regarding my loved one. It's one of those memories triggered by something else, and today it was about the coffee.

When my loved one worked in San Francisco, the corner Starbuck barista would see him walking by the front window. By the time he was at the front of the line, his coffee was made without him even ordering the venti cappuccino with three raw sugars. Even though he wasn't into food, he surely loved his coffee.

Once he was too ill to work, he managed to find his way into the kitchen just to make his coffee. He was a big fan of fine coffees, and he would make a pot that was so dark that I often questioned how many spoonsful of coffee actually went into the pot. But as his health declined, so did the amount of coffee he drank. I noticed the last year of his life that he rarely had more than two cups per day and they were spread hours apart.

One day I saw a trail of drops on the floor leading from the kitchen to his chair in the living room. I immediately saw the coffee cup and found myself irritated, wondering why he hadn't cleaned up his mess. We had a conversation about it, but he was oblivious that anything had spilled. He promised to be careful. But once you notice something, you can't "un-notice" it. Now I found myself on a daily hunt for the drops of coffee, and of course, if you hunt for something, you eventually find it. I had to think about why I was irritated as I knew it wasn't deliberate. He was sick, physically shook, and used a walker, so I decided not to say anything, to just let it go. I realized that my anger was about his illness and not about the drops of coffee.

As I sat at the drive-up window and picked up my cappuccino, I was grateful that I didn›t say anything on that long-ago day. I decided to let it go because I didn›t want my memories filled with arguments over something so insignificant as drops of coffee or, worse, memories of my intolerance over the little things that my loved one did.

94

The Joy

"I don't have to chase extraordinary moments to find
happiness – it's right in front of me if I'm paying
attention and practicing gratitude."
~ Brene Brown

I went to a convention and was looking forward to hearing the Sunday morning spiritual speaker. She focused on living by spiritual principles to enhance our lives with love, joy, and acceptance. I can't remember the particulars of what she shared but what I do know is that I walked away feeling a bit lighter and grateful to have attended the event.

After checking out of the hotel, I drove home looking at the snow-covered scenery and letting my mind wander to the things that gave me some peace. Even though I get nervous driving on slippery roads, I felt blessed for my beautiful drive through the country.

The positive messages of the past three days filled my mind, providing the relief that I so craved. I flashed to the previous week and how much I thought about canceling but eventually gave in to my faith and trust that all would be fine. I believed that I would have an opportunity to escape my sadness for a little while and, at

195

this moment, was so grateful that I stayed.

I was grateful for:

- The ability to get out of myself and my self-pity.
- My friends showed compassion by spending time with me.
- The faith that gets me through my life.
- A sense of contentment with my current life.
- A job that provides me a place to feel useful.
- The possibility of a life with meaning.

Upon entering my house, I immediately made a fire and sat on the chaise to contemplate the feelings of the last three days. At this moment, I am overwhelmed with gratitude to have returned home feeling this kind of joy and peace in my heart.

95

The Blessings

"Social media has given us this idea that we should all have a posse of friends when in reality, if we have one or two really good friends, we are lucky."
~ Brene Brown

With my significant other being sick, I found it challenging to be available to others, let alone be a friend. I was overwhelmed with my 'To Do' list, which contained everything that had to be done to ensure he was taken care of while I worked and traveled. Unfortunately, that list was extensive and did not include spending time making friends or showing up for the few I already had.

But, one day, I woke up and realized that my life was not what I thought it should be, and, at that moment, I knew I had to do something different. Even though my life was filled with all the have to's I began to make a concerted effort to change how we had been living. My approach changed from avoiding people at all costs to saying 'yes' when asked to participate. As we allowed people into our lives and our home, we found ourselves enjoying life more.

As the years passed, our lives were enriched with joy, food, parties, and bonfires because of these friends: these blessings. These friends were the ones who showed up with phone calls, visits, food, and just to keep us company.

The testament of true friendship is that true friends show up when life gets hard. They showed up after my loved one passed, knowing that there would be plenty of uncomfortable moments filled with tears, stories of grief, loneliness, and unbearable sadness.

At this time in my life, I find myself with fewer acquaintances and just a handful of friends, but these friends are the ones that came and continue to come to support and love me in my grief. Their showing up illustrates what true blessings are, and today I know that I am not alone and that a kind and loving spirit is working in my life. I am blessed.

96

The Acting as If

"I see my path, but I don't know where it leads. Not knowing where I'm going is what inspires me to travel it."
~ Rosalia de Castro

I had never heard of the phrase 'acting as if' until a friend spoke about it at a support group meeting. After many years this term has become one of the most effective tools I've learned to use in my life. In the beginning, it provided me with a way of trusting that I could do something or believe in something that didn't seem possible – just by acting as if I could.

I have utilized this concept through the years when confronted with things I found difficult. When I was unable to connect with a god of my understanding, I acted as if I had one, and working with my spiritual mentor, I developed one that I was comfortable with.

When I was diagnosed with cancer many years ago, I acted as if I could get through the moment, the next biopsy, the next is surgery, and, as a result, my attitude got me through a tough time in my life.

'Acting as if' is the temporary answer I often seek. The concept gets me through this moment where all I feel is pain, fear, confusion, or lack of trust. This moment when I think I can't go on. If I act as if I am fine and I can stay in the present, I am ok, both with myself and the world around me. I have found that when I do this, my insides eventually come to match what I had been projecting.

Why is this concept important as I struggle with grief? Based on my previous experiences, perhaps this concept will work on my feelings as I walk through the loss of my loved one. My past has shown me that when I do so, I come to believe that I would and could get to the other side of the feelings or the circumstances threatening to overwhelm me. This didn›t mean that everything would be wonderful. It simply meant that I would be given enough hope to get through the moments of anger, remorse, and despair I was feeling in my grief.

It had been a while since my loved one passed, and I found myself in the process of making a life without him. So I began reminding myself to just act as if I would make it another day without my loved one. Somehow, this acting helped me muster enough hope and faith that I would be given the courage to get to the next day. Trusting that if I continued to act as if I would be fine. I am beyond grateful for this concept as I trust it will help with my grief and provide hope that I don›t need to know my destination, but I will be just fine when I arrive.

97

The Guilty Good Time

"Well, I'm having a good time. Which makes me feel
guilty too. How very English."
~ David Attenborough

The summer before my husband's passing centered around physician visits, hospitalizations, and nurses coming to the house. But in the middle of this, I would fantasize about my loved one and me going to the theater. It was a great fantasy as it felt very grown up, sophisticated, and quite different from our day-to-day reality. The summer seemed to drag on, but we both hoped to enjoy our season tickets – especially Chekhov's 'Man in a Case' starring Mikhail Baryshnikov. However, as the summer ended, all hope of us attending this play together also ended.

After his passing, I invited a friend who loved musicals and dance to attend 'Man in the Case.' She gladly accepted the invite, and we made plans for the evening.

Saturday night. As I dressed for the theater, I realized that I was excited about the evening's festivities. I met my friend, and over dinner, we talked about our day-to-day lives, work, children, and our excitement about seeing Mikhail Baryshnikov. We entered the theater, and the excitement was palpable. Everyone seemed wholly engaged in the evening's promise. From the time the lights dimmed and the curtain rose, we were in another world and another time. When the play ended, we said our goodbyes and went separate ways.

Driving home, I was happy for my evening. It occurred to me that it had been a long time since I felt the excitement of doing something different, something enjoyable. And then it hit me that I had actually had a good time – and I did not once think of my husband. The guilt immediately consumed me, and I wanted to cry.

It had been five months since my loved one passed, and this was the first time that I forgot to think of him. I had been looking forward to this play for a long time, so I decided not to ruin my experience with guilt tonight. In fact, that guilt helped me remember who my loved one really was. He wasn't resentful or petty. If he had been too sick to attend, he would have encouraged me to go without him. I know he would want me to enjoy the play, so I let the thoughts of this enjoyable evening wash over me.

98

The Other Widows

*"When one person says, 'Yeah, me, too,' it gives
permission for others to open up."*
~ Tarana Burke

I felt alone and worse, as if no one really understood how
difficult these past days had been. I found myself killing time and
pretending to walk through my life when I knew that I was not.
Earlier in my grief, a woman came up to me and shared that she
had lost her husband to an illness, and for a brief moment, I knew I
wasn't alone. But as soon as she walked away, the feeling faded.

Knowing that I needed to take care of myself, I would go to
my support group wrapped in my grief cocoon, not hearing much
of what others were sharing. There were sessions where all I would
do was cry and couldn't wait to leave. Despite my feelings, I knew
I wasn't alone. I needed to get out of my head and listen to where
others were in their grief process.

Self-pity had gotten hold of me, and I needed to do something
different, so I got myself out of the house and went to a party at
a friends' home. When I entered, the hostess approached me and
promptly introduced me to two women who had lost their husbands. One of the women had lost her loved one five years before

and the other within the last year.

Spending some time talking with these women reminded me of the strength that comes with sharing our stories. They both emphasized their continued commitment to self-care and surrounding themselves with support. Knowing that I wasn't alone was the beginning, and the women sharing how they were surviving, thriving, dealing with their children, and working gave me hope.

When they were done, I knew that getting out of myself long enough to come to the party was an attempt at self-care. Separating myself from my grief and meeting these two widows was a blessing. It provided me with the recognition that I wasn›t alone and could get to the other side. As fate would have it by attending this party, I was allowed to be at the right place, at the right time to hear the right message.

99

The Recognition

"'Widow' is a word I never thought would describe me,
but I had to learn to deal with that."
~ Eve Arden

Looking in the dictionary for a definition of the word widow I read that it was a woman whose husband had died and remained unmarried. That was the black and white, to the point, and accurate depiction. But what the dictionary didn't do was describe the feelings that go along with the word.

It wasn't only that he had died; it was the previous twenty years of uncertainty, illness, and fear that contributed to my current state of mind. Five months had gone by, and it didn't seem possible that I was surviving the feelings I experienced. It felt like I had lived through a war – a very intimate war – one that no one understood.

I remembered a woman I'd met through a friend, the one whose husband had passed after a long illness. Feeling desperate, I called her. We had several conversations, and she seemed open and comfortable listening to me. When she shared parts of her story, her experience provided me with a window into a possible future where hope existed. She showed me that maybe I could survive.

During one of our conversations, she said she would be traveling to New York on business. I immediately took the opportunity to invite her to my home. After several months of speaking on the telephone, she arrived in New England.

Even though she was a stranger, it didn't feel that way. We hugged like old friends. She stayed a few days, and the relief I felt while she was in my home was a welcome change. She fanned the tiny flame of belief that things would change. I can never repay her kindness and willingness to share her story with me. It made a difference. This visit and her sharing helped replace a little of my fear with hope.

I am reminded that I am never the only one to go through life's experiences. If I am lucky, I can always find someone else, and, even better, they will bless us both by sharing that experience with me.

100

The Hanging On

"Life goes on if you're one of the lucky ones."
~ Judy Blume

After months of crying, I was not only sad, but depression had set in. Deep in my heart, I didn't believe that anyone could survive years of pain, fear, and the subsequent loss of a loved one. Even though I thought that others must have felt this way, I somehow still felt unique. And alone.

Somewhere I'd read that life goes on no matter what we have experienced. But, I did not believe it. The prospect of moving on was not at all attractive. A trusted friend told me that I just needed to hang on, and the intensity of the feelings would change. Somehow, the concept of hanging on long enough for me to believe that I could start feeling better seemed like a distant dream. But at least it was something positive to hold on to.

After just holding on, I started to experience moments of reprieve. I began noticing these moments during conversations with others when the focus wasn't on me or my experience. These moments of distraction came when I least expected them and often just by doing the day-to-day things: going into work, picking up groceries, ordering take out. The greatest reprieve came from being available to others and listening to their issues and their problems.

It took six months for me to begin noticing the moments of truce from my grief. These moments provided me with the faith that I could survive. Perhaps at some point, I would even begin to thrive. This realization strengthened my faith, and it reinforced my past experiences. I would get what I needed. All I had to do was show up for the next moment, hour, day, and I would be alright.

As I walk down my path, that far away dream of feeling better seems a little closer. I get small glimpses and moments where I see myself thriving, walking through my grief. The realization that when I am there for others, I feel better continues to help me. I know I am one of the lucky ones because now I can imagine that my life will go on and all I have to do is hang on long enough to see and to feel the change.

101

The Marble Jar

"My love can't be purchased…Best gifts have been
well-thought-out surprises."
~ Nina Dobrev

I woke up one morning with one thing in mind: beginning my spring cleaning. I made breakfast and sat at the dining room table, sipping on a diet cola and gazing into the backyard. The perennials were starting to bloom. It was a beautiful day, and it was clear that spring was here.

My sights were set on cleaning my little library. I started to re-move books and knickknacks from the shelves when I came upon a marble jar given to me by my loved one. The jar was one of several birthday gifts received five or six years before his death. I picked it up, began dusting, and decided to look inside.

As I opened the jar, I remembered all the little pieces of torn card stock and how each piece had a handwritten message in gold ink. One by one, I pulled out the pieces of paper and read the con-tents. His thoughts, love, and sense of humor were all in there with personalized messages just for me. The jar contained everything from the thirteen I Love You's to 'I couldn't find a dust buster.' However, when I got to the torn piece of paper with "Isn't this romantic?" the floodgates opened.

I sat in my library, reliving the memory of this birthday gift. When I first received all the presents, I remember that this marble jar was the one that I liked the least. Little did I know that of all the gifts to be received on that day, this would be the only one I would remember and the one that I cherish the most.

Reading through each piece of paper allowed me to embrace the memories of that day. I was painfully reminded of his absence; however, what was still there and what I clearly felt was his love for me.

102

The Welcoming Home

"My favorite thing is to have a big dinner
with friends and talk about life."
~ Carla Gugino

In my early twenties, I felt out of place everywhere. My parents lived out of the country, and the few invitations I received from family were uncomfortable. Having this conversation with our support group, my husband and I found that our professions had taken many of us to different states, away from family support.

Recognizing an almost universal theme, group members made a concerted effort to provide something that felt like support from family. Relationships were established; we were privileged to find people who became more like family than friends. We were invited to their birthday celebrations, holiday parties, and BBQs. They opened their hearts and welcomed us into their homes.

Moving to the northeast, we bought our first home, and we made a concerted effort to recreate the warmth and caring feeling we had been privileged to receive. We wanted to make sure that the people in our lives felt welcome, so we began to open our house up to others by having dinner parties, card games, and bonfires.

After my loved one passed, I was afraid the welcoming home

we had made would be gone forever. Neither the house nor my life felt the same without him. I realized that part of the reason my home didn't feel welcoming was because I literally had closed the door. I hadn't invited anyone into the house in quite a while. It became clear that I needed to open up my home. More importantly, I wanted to welcome our friends again.

Six months after my loved one passed, I invited a group of friends to come over for dinner and play cards. I made a lovely dinner, the friends brought snacks and dessert. After our tasty meal, we began our card game. As the evening passed, there was much conversation, teasing, smiles, and laughter that the house again began to feel like it had in the past – welcoming.

103

The Illusion, the Promise, the Ever After

"Death is not the greatest loss in life. The greatest loss is what dies inside us while we live."
~ Norman Cousins

No one gets through this life without experiencing bereavement. The loss of family members has been among my most difficult experiences. I have found that something inside of me profoundly changed with each one.

My father was the first significant loss of my life, and the only good thing surrounding his death was my ability to be there for him. Thanks to my employer, I was able to work out of my father's home. This enabled me to occasionally transport him to the doctor, chemotherapy, and radiation appointments. I worked hard to practice the spiritual principle of selflessness, which gave me the gift of five extra months with him and the privilege of being there for his last breath. Upon his passing, I experienced the death of the illusion that I was daddy's little girl. He was always there as my support, and even though I hadn't been his little girl in a very long time, the reality of never being anyone's little girl hit me hard.

After my father died, my mother and I began to speak daily. A deeper relationship began to emerge. So, when I lost her three years later to a brain aneurysm, I was heartbroken. The call from the hospital stated she was on life support. Despite my aching heart, I understood that the damage was extensive, and she was gone. I was present for her last breath, and I tried to focus on that privilege.

Nonetheless, I found myself deeply touched by her death. We had started having a close, more meaningful relationship; now, I felt an enormous loss. Something inside of me died with her. When I thought about it, I recognized the death of the promise that we would get even closer.

The loss of my husband has impacted me the hardest. He was my life's partner, the love of my life, and witnessing what he went through broke my heart. The last three weeks of his life were brutal as he struggled for every breath and heartbeat. After years of illness and pain, his life ended. But I was again blessed with the privilege of being there for my loved one's final breath. And I saw the promise that we would live happily ever after perish with him.

I have learned to look at these significant losses with a different set of eyes. I now recognize that what I thought of as the death of being daddy's little girl was an illusion. I can still feel the love he had for his little girl. When I think of the death of the promise that I would be closer to my mother, I realize that we were close. Her death isn't going to change that.

Finally, even though my loved one's physical life ended, it didn't extinguish his happily ever after. I realize that my ever after was shorter than expected, but I focus on the fact that we were happy when his ever after ended.

104

The Unknowns

"I don't have a gardener, because I enjoy pulling weeds. It's hard to explain, but there is something fulfilling about pulling out a weed and knowing that you got all the roots."
~ Justin Hartley

Getting my hands in the dirt gave me a purpose. For several years before my loved one's death, I had done minimal work in the yard, and everything was overgrown with unknowns. Getting the garden back in some sort of shape was the goal.

I set foot in the garden and began the slow process of pulling weeds, holding a vision in mind. When I started weeding, I found my moves were deliberate. After a while, I got lost in the moment, and I was just doing. I had no thoughts of sadness or happiness — only of weeds. I was able to get lost in physical activity. After a few hours, I saw the payoff for all my hard work; that gave me an overwhelming sense of peace. I had spent several hours in a meditative state, just listening to the sounds around me and enjoying the beauty of the sprouting plants.

I have always heard of the gifts that prayer and meditation can bring to our lives. However, meditation had always been something that I struggled with; it often eluded me. I lived with the preconceived notion that I needed to burn incense and play exotic music to meditate. I was grateful to discover I didn›t need a reading from one of my spiritual texts to connect. Nor was I required to burn incense, listen to music or even to believe in a specific religion. All I needed to get in touch with my inner voice was to be present and in the moment.

It was the middle of spring, and I was genuinely grateful to recognize that I meditated every time I worked in my garden. This had always been something that others could do, and now it turns out that just pulling the unknowns out of the ground was the simplest way for me to clear my mind, listen, and enjoy a feeling of peace.

105

The Reciprocity

"People are going to come into your life that need you, and being there for them makes the day worth living. People are going to come into your life that you need, and that's the really crazy thing."
~ Amy Grant

As a child in elementary school, I heard a teacher speak about The Golden Rule and the phrase "Do unto others as you would have them do unto you." The sentiment stuck with me, and I tried to carry it into all areas of my life as an adult. The wonderful thing about The Golden Rule is its simplicity and the concept of reciprocity. If I want respect, I have to give respect. If I want someone to show me empathy, caring, and love, I have to be willing to give empathy, caring, and love.

Through the years, I have been able to carry this simple rule into my dealings with others. My friendships placed high on my priority list, yet I became significantly closed off and self-centered in my grief. Being a friend taught me to be loyal, honest, non-judgmental, and trusting; because of this, I have some amazing friends. They listened when I cried, held me when I felt broken, brought me food when I stopped eating, and loved me when I was unlovable. And they did all of it without judgment.

I understood that to have friends I had to be one. As that thought entered my mind, I began to judge myself harshly for my inability to be a friend during that last year of my loved one's life. I was consumed with the day-to-day caretaking, which was a priority. But, after he passed, my behavior didn't change. The self-centered thoughts and actions continued. I realized how blessed I had been as these friends continued to be willing to reach out when I couldn't, wouldn't, or just was too overwhelmed to even think of being there for someone else. As I typed these words, a sense of shame washed over me. I could do better, and all I had to do was choose to change.

After seven months, I decided to show up for some fantastic people who let me be part of their lives. I started off small and took a few moments to ensure that their birthdays, anniversaries, and memorable moments were in my calendar. I also sent some delayed delivery emails to remind me to call certain people soon. Focusing on reciprocity has made taking these small steps easier, and I began to feel like a friend to these significant people in my life.

106

The Killing Time

"Nothing seems to me so likely to make people unhappy in themselves and at variance with others as the habit of killing time."
~ Dorothea Dix

Eight months after I lost my husband, I started to see a tiny bit of what my new life would be. A routine that had taken shape:

- Participating in my support group.

- Occasionally eating out with friends.

- Going to work.

- Finding ways to kill time.

I went to my support group a couple of times per week. That ate up a few hours. Sharing what I felt was helpful, but whatever reprieve I got lasted only a short while. I was soon back to trying to fill my day with anything just to get to the next one.

I attempted to meet my friends for dinner at least once per week. These meet-ups always provided me with the necessary entertainment and distraction as the women shared their weeks' dealings with their children, boyfriends, husbands, and jobs. I found myself wrapped up in their stories, providing me with an opportunity to get out of myself.

The biggest consumer of my time was my employment. I went to work every day and immersed myself in the minutia of research, writing, and delivering training. My days were filled with the busy, which seemed so important that I would often continue a project when I got home, working late into the evening. I'd spend endless hours doing the little things on a presentation to make it engaging and visually appealing for the participants. Killing time disguised as productivity.

I wanted to avoid being present in my life and was willing to do just about anything to ensure that I was absent. Searching for ways to kill time became a full-time job. I needed to learn to live my waking hours without filling them with the meaningless. In a moment of clarity, I realized I owe it to myself to stop searching for anything that will fill my time and instead just be, feel, and embrace what those moments are. I was empty, the kind of empty that comes from deep inside. I was uncomfortable. All I needed to do was to feel it without trying to fix it. My heart knows these feelings are appropriate and will eventually pass.

107

The Mowing

"I spend hours mowing the lawn in absolutely straight lines on my tractor. If it's not right, I do it again".
~ Britt Ekland

To enjoy the fabulous 85-degree weather that marked the Fourth of July holiday, I puttered around the yard, pulling weeds. I saw it was time to mow the one-acre lawn surrounding my house.

Going to the shed, I pulled out the tractor and started my mowing journey. Any time I sat on that tractor, my mind would wander. But on occasion, I was completely focused, and the act of sitting and mowing became meditative.

On this day, I thought about moving into our home nine years ago. Once we settled, I volunteered for lawn mower duty. He was simply too ill. We began searching for a mower I would feel comfortable and safe using. I looked at tractors and decided the property's hills and uneven terrain made me nervous. We came home with a self-propelled lawn mower that I thought would be sufficient.

We brought it home, filled it with gas, and I began pulling on the starter rope. After several tries, it became apparent that I wasn't strong enough to get it going, so my loved one stepped in. He also had a difficult time but eventually turned the engine over. Afraid it would stall out, I immediately started mowing. Grabbing the lawnmower, I made my way up the closest hill, huffing and puffing all the way to the top. When I turned around to come down the hill, I saw my loved one laughing hysterically. Once I reached the bottom, I saw no grass catcher. I'd never attached it in my rush to get started and was covered from head to toe with the tiny green pieces of grass.

I continued mowing my lawn and immediately smiled as I pictured what my loved one saw – the human chia pet. We eventually traded the self-propelled mower for a tractor. I am still so grateful that we had the little mower because it gave me another humorous memory. I have found that through my grief process, I often don't remember our many shared moments where humor, laughter, and just joy were felt. This has now become one of my favorites. As silly as this memory was, it made me connect to that part of our relationship that hasn't come up very often since his death. Right now, I hold it tight.

108

The Couples

"It's not the same without Jerry. It never will be."
~ Bill Kreutzmann

Deciding to get married when we were older necessitated some thought because of our previous relationship experiences. I was a single thirty-eight-year-old mother with one child and had chosen to never marry. My loved one had been married twice before and had three children. So, the question was, what were we doing and why?

When we started dating, I paid particular attention to how he dealt with my son and me. I wasn't married, but I definitely wasn't the average single person. My son and I were a package, and he needed to understand that. We dated for nine months, and we shared our stories which brought us closer. As time passed, we accepted each other – the good, the bad, and the ugly. The most important factor we discovered was that we were in love and wanted to make this commitment because we had finally found someone to share our lives with.

Being in love and making a lifetime commitment was a step that I thought I would never make. But here I was – ready, willing, and trusting that this was the right move. We would forever be known as Ron and Rosina, the couple from this point forward. The couple who in the end had spent twenty years together – through thick and thin. Together no matter what. But after his death, being just Rosina sounded incomplete. The couple was no longer, and I was having difficulty adjusting to just being the solitary me.

After his death, I felt blessed to have had a couple of months to be oblivious to the others around me. But then I started to notice other couples, the couples of which I was no longer one. Everywhere I looked, they were there – couples going out to dinner, attending a party, or just going to the movies. I struggled with my grief when I was alone. This had changed, and now I noticed the couples around me with a mix of grief and a touch of envy which made me feel unbelievably small and petty.

However, a few months later, I caught a glimpse of an older couple holding hands and taking a stroll through the mall. There was something special about the image. They seemed happy, in love, and I realized how fortunate they were to still be together. I found myself filled with gratitude that I recognized their love. I found that I could momentarily let go of my grief and envy to allow this image to enter my heart. And just for that moment, I felt a little peace.

109

The Picture

"A photograph is a moment – when you press the button,
it will never come back."
~ Rene Burri

My daughter and son searched for the appropriate picture of their father for his obituary, wake, and funeral services. After searching his computer, they found one where he had a small smile. It was printed, framed, and placed beside the coffin for his wake and funeral services. Afterward, the framed picture was brought back to our home and put on his office couch along with everything else from that terrible day.

Within a few days, I hung the picture in his office, even though it made me really sad. I assumed that I would get used to seeing the image on the wall; however, I did not. Every time I walked by his office, I saw the picture. It only made me sadder, more uncomfortable, and frankly, I hated it. All this picture did was remind me that he was gone, so I removed it from the wall and put it in the closet. I thought that removing this picture would bring some relief, but the realization hit me that all pictures with his image made me sad. So, I walked around my house, collected every picture of him, and put them all in his closet.

Time passed. I began to heal enough that I started searching for a picture of us enjoying our lives, where he wasn't too ill, and where happy memories flourished. Pulling out the pictures from the closet, I looked at them with a critical eye and found none of them to be of happy moments, so I continued my search.

Nine months after his death, I traveled to spend time with our daughter. Looking around her home, I found a picture we had sent to her. The image captured a surprise cruise to celebrate his 60th birthday where we were all dressed up waiting for our dinner. I remembered the chocolate-covered strawberries delivered to our room, the lovely dinners we shared, us dancing. But the best part was sitting on our private balcony watching the stars in the evening. Asking permission to remove the picture and bring it back, I felt some peace. My search for a picture that captured a happy us was over. When I got home, I found the perfect place for it.

When I sit in my library reading or thumbing through a magazine, all I have to do is glance up and see the smiles on our faces. The picture immediately takes me to the beautiful place where we were happy and now I can have hope that more lovely memories will return to my life.

110

The Unattended Concert

"Complete strangers can stand silent next to each other in an elevator and not even look each other in the eye. But at a concert, those same strangers could find themselves dancing and singing together like best friends. That's the power of music."
~ LZ Granderson

Music was always something that my loved one and I had in common. Even though the genres we enjoyed were different, we loved listening to music at home, in the car, and especially live. Some of my fondest memories continue to be our evenings out at a favorite restaurant followed by a concert. Attending these concerts was a fantastic shared experience and one of the many joys of our marriage.

We both needed something to anticipate. Knowing how much he loved concerts and how tenuous his health was, we made an effort to buy tickets several months in advance. However, as his illness progressed, we found that accommodations needed to be made: a place to rest, oxygen, and wheelchair access so we could continue to enjoy going out. Sometimes these accommodations made things difficult and so complex that we could not attend. But we continued to try, and most of the time, we were able to enjoy

227

the evening out.

My loved one was dead set on attending a particular rock concert in a beautiful outside amphitheater situated in a field of pine and oak trees. We both loved the bands that were playing, So, I bought two wheelchair-accessible tickets, and the countdown for this next adventure began. However, two weeks before the concert, he came down with pneumonia. He never got better.

On the anniversary of what would have been that last rock concert, I held those unused tickets in my hand, and feelings of loss immediately surfaced. I recognized that he is not only gone from my life but apparently so is the music that had once filled it. It's funny how it took so long to notice that music was missing from my life. I summoned the courage to do something different, got on my computer, and found a concert I wanted to attend. I clicked the purchase button, even though it was two months away, I found myself smiling. What occurred to me is something I can keep from my earlier life: just like before, I can have something to look forward to.

111

The Call from HR

*"There is never just one thing that leads to success for anyone.
I feel it is always a combination of passion, dedication,
hard work, and being in the right place at the right time."*
~ Lauren Conrad

Working in a big corporation, I knew it was important to show continued interest in and willingness to pursue growth opportunities. I told my direct supervisor that I wanted to explore upper management positions. Still, when I discovered no current openings, I was instructed to write a proposal for a stretch opportunity and submit it to several vice presidents for consideration. To my surprise, they approved my proposal, so I made flight and hotel arrangements to experience this potential future job.

I spent a week shadowing the person currently holding the position in another office. It was a thought-provoking week, and I learned a lot about myself and the job. The moment I set foot on the plane to return home, I knew that it was too soon to try anything new. During the four- and half-hour flight, I found myself slipping back into depression. I knew I could function and do well at my current position, but anything additional was overwhelming. So, I asked myself why I had bothered to go cross country to see this position? I understood I needed to demonstrate my willingness to try something new, but I wasn't ready.

Returning to the office, my supervisor had scheduled a meeting to discuss my stretch experience. As we began speaking, it became clear that I was not okay. I was distraught and depressed and whatever words I used to express my feelings caught her off guard. She immediately started assessing if I was a danger to myself and contacted Human Resources. I spent the next half hour vehemently denying any suicidal thoughts and convincing them that I would not hurt myself. After the meeting, I went back to my desk feeling so vulnerable that I packed my computer and left the office, managing to avoid everyone on my way out the door.

It had been nine months since the loss of my loved one, and I was shocked that I was unaware of how others were perceiving me. I cried for a while, but I couldn't let go of what had happened. On the drive home, I telephoned my psychiatrist, shared what had happened, and convinced him that I would be fine until our next appointment. When I arrived home, I was physically tired, angry, and vulnerable.

I just wanted to crawl into bed. Instead, I sat in the three-season room and looked at the woods, which typically provided some relief from the pain. Not that day. I prayed for a bit of peace, and as I made dinner, I understood that taking a small step into self-care was the best I could do today. And that was fine.

112

The Harm

"The difference between the almost right word and the right word is really a large matter – 'tis the difference between the lightning–bug and the lightning."
~ Mark Twain

Depending on the day's mood, this first year has either flown by or has dragged on. I tried not to lash out or harm others, but deep in my heart, I knew that I had. While I try to be kind most of the time, I'd been short with others. Despite being a caring and compassionate person, I had been inconsiderate and self-centered. Worst of all, there had been times that I made no attempt to contain my self-righteous anger. It was as if I felt entitled to share my misery with others.

I always knew when I was not acting in a manner consistent with my spiritual values. All that needed to happen was to dislike what was said or done, or sadly, even what was not said. My flaws would rear their ugly heads in the most shameful ways, adding a layer of remorse on top of the self-pity.

I'm embarrassed to say that I was at a grocery store and realized I was both impatient with the checkout person and felt the need to verbalize my displeasure, belittling her. I was ashamed to see how tightly I was holding on to the bitterness embedded in my heart.

I got ready for bed, inventoried my day, and thought of the people that had crossed my path. If I was unkind, I tried to figure out a way to make things right. Sometimes just going back and saying, "I'm sorry" is all the amends needed. However, I knew that often things could not be made right with an apology. In that case, the best I could do was focus on not repeating the harmful behavior.

Ten months had passed since my loved one died, and I was aware of the pain I had caused others. I choose not to repeat the impatience, unkind words, or misdirected anger that made me feel bad about myself.

I committed to using care with how I spoke to or about others. And to interact with them more mindfully. Making this commitment gave me an opportunity to fix my past behaviors and the blessing to live my future with continued living amends to those I had harmed. I've realized that being a widow did not give me license to walk through life being angry, resentful, or just plain mean. So, this day marked a new and healthier beginning.

Intellectually, I know that just because a thought comes into my head, it doesn't need to exit via my mouth. Not only do I not need to share that ugly thought, but I also might not even have the right to do so. It doesn't matter that I am a widow in pain, nor does it matter that my life is different than I'd hoped. Facts? Yes. But these facts cannot be used as an excuse to mistreat others.

I am at the beginning of one of the most challenging times in my life, and doing the next right thing will help keep me from living with additional shame over my behavior. I am reminded that acting with tolerance, compassion, and restraint brings peace to my heart. I sleep better and feel better about who I am.

113

The Mentor's Direction

"The direction of your focus is the direction your life will move. Let yourself move toward what is good, valuable, strong and true."
~ Ralph Marston

Challenging times can sometimes enhance the illusion that I can do everything alone. I know I will be fine. However, this opens the door to a difficult and dangerous mindset: I don't need anyone.

When I allow self-will to take over, I stop reaching out to my friends. I especially stop reaching for my spiritual mentor. Obviously, this diminishes any possibility of getting unbiased input on my issues. Finding myself in this pattern, I needed to reach out and stop avoiding the people and information that would help me move on with my life.

Before my loved one's passing, I worked on some journaling that helped me look at my past actions and avoid harming others with my words or deeds. I hadn't looked at this writing since his death. It was time to continue and to reach out to my mentor.

I arranged to meet her, and as I shared my writing, I experienced a sense of relief simply from getting together to talk. I was accountable in all areas of my life, and I communicated what I had done in the past to cause harm to others. As I shared my writing, I realized I had done damage to my loved one. There was shame around sharing this particular harm because I felt so petty. She didn't judge and just listened as I spoke. Occasionally she would share some insight or suggest actions to let go and move on.

Having finished our conversation, she gave me two things to do. Prayer sets the stage for healing, so the first thing she told me to do was to pray for those I had harmed – including my loved one and myself. The second was to change my behavior – to stop isolating and share with my support system no matter what.

So today, my priority is to be kind to others and practice compassion. I believe that natural healing can now begin and release some of the hurt in my heart.

114

The Wedding Ring

"I don't ever really feel that wearing my wedding ring is what determines me being married or not."
~ Jessica Simpson

I went to a celebration, and a woman in attendance shared that she had been widowed less than six months. As I glanced down at her hand, I noticed that she no longer wore a wedding ring. I watched her interact with the people in the room and specifically with the men. She seemed outgoing, gregarious, and warm. She was in a place that I couldn't even imagine with my eleven months of widowhood.

After seeing her, I sat and looked at my hand and the hand of every other married woman. I thought about what being married truly meant, so I grabbed a dictionary and found the words united, interconnected, joined, and intimately combined were used to define marriage.

We went from two individuals with two families to one slightly dysfunctional family. We were fortunate to be able to unite and combine these two entities. Being married and having that kind of commitment meant that we shared our entire lives: the good, the bad, and the occasionally ugly. As a direct result, our lives became fuller, stronger, more complicated, sometimes happier, and ulti-mately more caring.

The year anniversary of his death was looming, and I wrestled with the thought of removing my wedding ring. For most people, the ring signifies that you are married and are living with a partner. I am just reminded that he is gone. We combined our lives when we took our vows, and even though he is gone, I still have that life. I have a home we built together, memories of our time shared, and children who have grown and have lives of their own. I still have the results of all the work we did to create a fuller, more robust, happier, and more loving life. Today, my ring is still on my finger because I am still married. For me, being married is more than having my partner – today, it includes having the life we shared.

115

The Biggest Gift

"To give somebody your time is the biggest gift you can give."
~ Franka Potente

For my birthday each year, my husband designed and created a homemade card. Every year, I looked forward to seeing what the year's birthday card would bring. One year it would be flowery and loved-filled, and another, it would be sarcastic and funny. But this year's card would only be what my imagination could construct.

It had been three hundred and twenty-seven days since my loved one passed. I woke up knowing that I only wanted to stay in bed. I had been thinking of this day for a week, projecting about how awful it would be. Knowing there was no homemade card from him broke my heart just a little more. I knew that I would lose the day in terrible self-pity if I continued down this path. So, before climbing out of bed, I said a prayer and asked for the courage to face my day and the ability to focus on all the things for which I am grateful.

By starting my gratitude list, I began to feel better. I was grateful for my children, home, friends, and the love I felt from a higher power. I got on my computer and saw that many friends had acknowledged my birthday and were happy I was part of their lives.

I was especially grateful for my birthday plans with a close friend. She had invited me to dinner, so I knew that I would be both distracted and in good company.

We had made plans to meet at one of my favorite restaurants, but when we arrived, it was closed. We chose another, and at our next stop, we were greeted, seated, and given menus. As the minutes passed, I found myself getting angrier and, after 45 minutes with no service, we left. Going to dinner was supposed to be a reprieve from my negativity, but our plans weren't working out. I just wanted to retreat into my cocoon.

My friend insisted however that we try one more place and our next stop was a little takeout dive right down the street. We placed our orders, and when the food was ready, we sat, ate, and talked. I realized that my friend had not only taken me out to celebrate my birthday, but she had given me the most significant gift of all -- her time. What I knew was that the day was not even close to being one of those perfect birthdays but, as I ended my day, I saw that I was loved. Despite my apprehension, I had been taken care of one more time.

116

The Laughter

*"We need more kindness, more compassion, more joy, more
laughter. I definitely want to contribute to that."*
~ *Ellen DeGeneres*

Having tossed and turned all night, I welcomed the new day.
The moment I opened my eyes, I realized how long it had actually
been since I genuinely enjoyed myself. The reality was that it had
been a long time. I had learned that I could always do something
different to change my feelings, thoughts, or situation. I searched
my memory for the last time I had such a great night, and one
recollection immediately popped into my head.

Before my loved one's death, a small group of friends gathered
at our home to play cards. Even though playing cards was not his
thing, he certainly enjoyed the company, food, conversations, and
all the laughter around the dining room table. Everyone had a
wonderful time, and the evening was filled with the posturing and
trash talk about who was going to be the evening's winner or, more
importantly, who would be the LOSERS. Having that memory
nudged me to decide that it was time to try something different. I
got on the phone and invited a handful of friends to come over on
the upcoming Saturday for dinner and cards.

It was the beginning of a very long week, and even though there was plenty of work that had to be done, I was in a surprisingly good mood. All I did was make a few phone calls, and my mood changed. The expression 'move a muscle to change a thought' works. By doing something different, I looked forward to being around others and anticipating that I would have a wonderful time.

When Saturday night came, I was ready for the evening. I did several things in advance to enjoy every part of the day. Fresh flowers were placed on the first floor, the dinner table was set for eight, all the prepared food was in the fridge, and the cards were ready to be dealt. As the evening approached, my mood lightened in anticipation of the conversations and laughter that would inevitably happen. I had really missed the laughter and was finally willing to reopen this door so it could return.

117

Rock Concert

"There's nothing better than live music. It's raw energy,
and raw energy feeds the soul."
~ Dhani Jones

It had been almost a year since my loved one passed. I chose my outfit as if I had stepped out of my past. I put on my Dr. Martens, a very short dress – or was it a shirt? My hair and nails were done, and I was ready to be surrounded by other music fans.

Getting in my car and driving to the arena, I noticed how long it had been since I felt that kind of excitement. I knew traffic would be terrible, parking would try my patience, and finding my solo seat would be uncomfortable. All those feelings disappeared when I realized how much I looked forward to going to this concert. It was a big event with 10,000 other people. Once in my seat, I actually started enjoying the insanity of the crowd. Being able to interact with people around me was fantastic, and as the stage lights dimmed, the screaming began, and I knew I was in the right place.

I had purchased the concert ticket months before. The headlining rock band was one I'd seen several times during my twenties, and thirty-plus years later, I was thrilled just to be part of the crowd. I felt wholly present and embraced my surroundings.

241

The music began, and many of us rushed the stage. I wanted to get a look at the musicians who had provided the memories that filled my past. To see the musicians and hear their performance was wonderful. Attending this concert allowed me to take a break from the heaviness of the last year despite missing my loved one. I wasn't sure what the night would bring, but I welcomed a reprieve from my thoughts, and it was just what the doctor ordered.

In hindsight, I discovered that I had completely let go of my anger, pain, and depression. Those constant companions had been replaced by the joy and lightheartedness of the music. This was the first concert since my loved one's death, and I had chosen to go alone. I knew that this was part of my starting over. Even though obtaining only one ticket was uncomfortable, I needed to make arrangements to get out of myself and just enjoy the music. Perhaps the next time I will bring a friend.

118

The Spark and the Passion

"My mission in life is not merely to survive, but to thrive;
and to do so with some passion, some compassion,
some humor, and some style."
~ Maya Angelou

Before my loved one's death, one of the bright spots in my life was work. I had been very fortunate to work at a job I loved. It provided me with an outlet to share my technical expertise and be somewhat creative in delivery. I enjoyed the opportunity to develop training materials. Even better, I facilitated classes, engaged our staff, and shared my passion for the work.

However, returning to work was difficult. I did my job to the best of my ability. Still, it was hard to concentrate and extremely taxing to project enthusiasm when I struggled to show up. Yet, it didn't matter what I was going through as the students needed to be engaged, and I merely needed to fake it until my enthusiasm came back.

As the months passed, I found myself coming back to life. The spark that had been missing began to reappear, and I started enjoying the activities in the class. To get mentally prepared before walking into a class, I'd say a quick prayer, enter the room acting as

243

if everything was fine, and then I'd just pretend.

On one of my week-long west coast business trips, I made my way to the office, admiring the beautiful scenery and smiling as I drove the rental. Even though I was tired from the flight, I realized I enjoyed setting up the classroom. I rearranged the tables, set flip charts around the room, and placed a name card and manual by each chair. Even though I had a long evening reviewing materials ahead, I was filled with joy and gratitude. It had taken almost a year, but the spark and passion I had experienced in the past was back.

119

The Impromptu Tour Guide

"It's usually a jolly good trick to pick up a local tour guide.
They can tell you all the anecdotes that make a place interesting.
I'm one for rushing off to museums at the crack of dawn,
eating fabulous things on terraces for lunch, and
long dinners on balmy evenings."
~ Jane Birkin

Life definitely goes on. Having returned to my employment, I worked with a colleague hired while I was on short-term disability. We spent some months working together, reviewing and updating the materials for our upcoming class in the San Francisco Bay area. This would be my first business trip since the death of my loved one, and I would be returning to what used to be our home. I felt a little apprehensive. Despite this, my colleague and I had several conversations about the trip, and I assured her that we would definitely spend some time in the city.

We arrived on Sunday and drove straight to the office to set up the classroom in preparation for our week. We knew it would be busy and the first couple of days were a blur. But on Wednesday, my colleague and I decided that as soon as the workday ended, we would go into the city and I would begin my impromptu tour guide responsibilities.

I had a good idea where to take her. Having lived inland, my loved one and I had ventured into the city many times. We'd walked around the streets as tourists, gone to parades, and had lovely meals in China and Japan towns. But on this occasion, the goal was to show my colleague as much of San Francisco as I possibly could in one evening.

We took the train into the city and I followed the exact tour that my loved one had given me when we moved to this area. We took the obligatory Powell and Market Cable Car passing Lombard Street, went to Ghirardelli Square, where we ate dinner at McCormick Seafood while overlooking Alcatraz Island. We then walked to Pier 39 to look at the seals, have ice cream, and back to the train and our hotel.

I clearly saw the joy on my colleague›s face throughout this adventure. She smiled ear to ear for hours. It occurred to me that this must have been what my loved one saw with me. This brought a smile to my face. It warmed my heart to be able to share this beautiful city with another person, all because he had been my tour guide.

120

The Welcome to Fall Party

"Autumn is a second spring when every leaf is a flower."
~ Albert Camus

In New England, autumn was something to celebrate. This gave us the excuse to host a Welcome to Fall party where food was plentiful, and everyone seemed to enjoy laughter and conversation around a bonfire. This was something my loved one and I truly enjoyed, and we looked forward to hosting it every year. It usually took place in early October. But, during the last year of his life, he had been too sick to even consider it. In fact, I was so consumed by his illness and subsequent death, I did not even notice that autumn had arrived.

The year following his death, I decided to host the annual Welcome to Fall party. This year I needed to have a celebration, to open my home to our friends, and welcome this beautiful time of year together. The planning began early, and I wanted this occasion to celebrate his life, make new memories, and share my love of him with those in attendance. In anticipation of this event, invitations were made and given to our friends. I began to get excited over the gathering. As I spoke with others, they, too, shared how excited they were and offered to help in any way that I needed.

The second Saturday in October came quickly. My day began early by pulling out the party tables, table cloths, chafing dishes, and torches. I set up the yard with benches and began preparing the food. A friend dropped off beautiful pumpkin vases that she created filled with wildflowers gathered from her woods. Once the flowers were placed around the tables, the house was ready for the evening's festivities.

The guests began arriving at four with food, drinks, flowers, and even wood for the bonfire. Everyone was exceedingly thoughtful, and the party was enjoyed by all.

There were many blessings on that day. It began with the beautiful scenery and the autumn colors. I was able to hear how our friends were affected by knowing him. Sitting by the bonfire surrounded by others in the crisp evening hours, the warmth from the fire felt wonderful. I was able to walk through a little more healing due to the support from our guests. But the most important thing that happened was I got a glimpse of a potential new life and the realization that perhaps my new life was worth having, living, and enjoying. I laid my head on my pillow with a heart full of gratitude.

121

The Path to You

"I truly believe that everything that we do and everyone that we meet is put in our path for a purpose. There are no accidents; we're all teachers – if we're willing to pay attention to the lessons we learn, trust our positive instincts and not be afraid to take risks or wait for some miracle to come knocking at our door."
~ Marla Gibbs

The one year anniversary of my loved one's death was fast approaching, and I was amazed at the realization that I had survived. I continued to put one foot in front of the other, understanding that some days are better than others. Surprisingly, not all of it had been painful. There were days when I wantcd to erase the years of bad memories, but then I was reminded that doing so would also erase the good. I didn't want to let go of the good: I survived twenty years of illness, emergency rooms, hospitals, and the horrible unmanageability of waiting for the other shoe to drop because of the love we shared.

A couple of months before his death, he wanted me to see what he had changed on his website. It was a page dedicated to me. I barely glanced at the page when the discomfort hit. The opening began with Gertrude Stein's "Rose is a rose is a rose is a rose." When I saw the word 'sainthood,' my ability to view the page abruptly ended. As uncomfortable as I was, I didn't want him to think that it wasn't appreciated, so I thanked him. However, the discomfort stuck with me as it was his deathbed confession and I was not ready to hear it.

After the year anniversary of his death, I summoned the courage to visit his website and the page he dedicated to me. What I found took my breath away as it was his unique way of expressing his love for me. There were words conveying courage, durability, and then he stated that I was his life's love. I again wasn't ready to read everything he had written and quickly exited the page. What stuck to me this time was that it was not a deathbed confession but instead an homage to me. I am so grateful that the love he conveyed there put me on track to feel his love.

122

The Not Knowing

"The only true wisdom is in knowing you know nothing."
~ Socrates

I spent the last three years of my loved one's life focused on what had to be done and emotionally preparing myself for his death. However, what I hadn't thought about was what my life would be like without him. This reality left me vulnerable and insecure, with a deep understanding of how much I really don't know. I started sharing with a close friend that I had no idea what I was doing and how uncomfortable my new normal was.

Before my husband's death, I shared with a friend how I survived losing my father, mother, and another close relative. Having experienced these losses, I thought I would know how to handle my husband's passing. Reality took me to a new depth of awareness and pain. That my feelings changed from one moment to the next left me unbalanced and, on occasion, entirely lost. Yes, I had expected to have feelings, but I also thought that I would handle whatever life was going to bring my way. That's not what has occurred.

The anniversary of my loved one's death was fast approaching, and I didn't know what was coming my way. I didn't know what to expect. I didn't know how to feel. I didn't have a clue as to what challenges would present themselves. I don't profess to have any answers but what I do know is that I have faith that whatever experiences I have gone through have not been in vain. Someday I will have an opportunity to share these experiences. Hopefully, they will bring a little solace to the next person who finds themselves suffering the loss of the love of their life.

123

The Year

"It was very hard for all of us. It's still very hard. The anniversary of his death just passed, and every single one of his friends, still, after all these years...it's unbelievable."
~ Eydie Gorme

365 days. 12 months. 52 weeks. 525,600 minutes. 7,358,400 breaths. 31,536,000 seconds since my loved one died. This was the first anniversary of his death. Even as I wrote these words calling it an anniversary sounded wrong. An anniversary calls for celebration; I assure you this did not.

I turned to my thesaurus and searched for something more appropriate. The words that I found included ceremony, commemoration, festival, jubilee, recurrence, occasion, remembrance, and milestone. On this day, I acknowledge a milestone.

Before even opening my eyes, I knew this day marked one whole year since I last held his hand, one year since I saw his blue eyes or heard his voice. I think back on that day and know he was suffering. He suffered more than anyone should and loved ones watched his passing suffered, too. He deserved an easier death, but as he used to say, "these are the cards I was dealt." I prayed that his transition was peaceful.

Three hundred sixty-five days ago I felt like I wouldn't survive my bereavement, certain that no one had experienced what I was going through. As the year progressed, I found myself ashamed for having feelings I couldn't control or hide. As the months passed, I found myself grabbing onto anything that could get me from one emotion to the next. I survived a year without hearing his voice, seeing his smile, or feeling his touch. I thought it would be impossible, but here I am.

So, what have I learned? I learned that I can survive my horrible feelings by feeling them. That a god of my understanding never left my side. I have more friends than I realized: they continued to reach out, show up and remind me that I was never alone. I learned that by working on spiritual principles, I could survive anything and I know in my heart that I did.

Another new beginning and was uneasy about starting another year without him. Sitting in my dining room, the phrase "a fresh start" popped into my head. This fresh start points to a place in the past that can now be released. Somewhere along the line mistakes were made, and this new beginning will correct them, allowing a new life to begin.

Still, I don't know what this fresh start will mean to me. Our life had some disappointments. I watched him suffer through multiple agonizing health crises and we didn't get enough time together, but I don't consider those disappointments a mistake to be corrected. The only thing I wanted to let go of was the emotional pain we endured through twenty years of illness.

As I write, I am reminded of a quote by Joseph Campbell, which says, "We must be willing to get rid of the life we've planned, so as to have the life that is waiting for us. The old skin has to be shed before the new one can come."

So, what's the life that is waiting for me? Today I'm aware that I fear what my future could bring, but I am willing to let that fear go and practice courage to allow my happiness. I have come to believe that I deserve a future filled with possibilities and the chance to be happy again.

It was three hundred and sixty-six days since my loved one passed, and this fresh start holds my commitment to practice the courage to be happy. I will embrace my unknown future; it will be filled with new experiences, new people, and the company of the loved ones who are still with me.

One of the most profound lessons life has ever taught me is that happiness cannot take the form of another person, place, or thing. All of those can easily be lost. Happiness has to come from within.

124

The Stain

*"When you come to my show, I want it to feel
like opera, like a theatre."*
~ *The Weekend*

It's funny how the mundane things in life can trigger a memory. I washed my car and decided to vacuum the back seat when a whitish stain caught my eye. This stain occurred when my loved one was transporting a gallon of white paint to prep for an upcoming art show. When he turned the wheel, the paint overturned and spilled into the back seat and floor of my brand-new car. I remember how sick he was and how hard he must have worked to clean this mess up before I came home from work.

For a month before the art show he had been working at getting some of his latest paintings framed, books and brochures printed and recruiting friends to assist with the actual setup in the gallery. On the other hand, I had made arrangements for a jazz trio to play and ordered appetizers for the guests during the opening.

Two days before the opening, my loved one and a couple of friends set up the gallery. The gallery was in a beautiful part of town with a view of a creek surrounded by woods. The show's installation was made difficult because hanging the paintings on the exposed brick walls was a challenge.

But when they were finished, the gallery looked amazing. His oil paintings were on the wall, photography in the bins, and poetry books displayed on a table.

On the day of the art opening, he was ill but anxious to greet the art patrons and our friends. The musicians played beautifully, he read a new poem to the crowd, and everyone seemed to have a nice time. He sold one large painting and a few of his photographs. When I think back on that day, I remember how appreciative he was over his friends supporting him, how beautiful the gallery looked, and knowing that he put his all into making the evening a success.

As I continued to vacuum the car, I saw the slight residue of white paint. All the effort, support, and energy put into the show paid off. It turned out to be his last one and has left me with a wonderful memory. I could have chosen to be upset over the stain in my new car and am so grateful I didn't; the memory of the evening is only filled with happiness.

125

The Beautiful Tree

"My fondest memories are generally the day after Thanksgiving.
I get the total decorating Christmas itch."
~ Katharine McPhee

Every year, the day after Thanksgiving was a day that I would look forward to. It meant that I could go to my local Christmas tree farm and start hunting that one unique tree. Black Friday was perfect for this one thing: not too early, but early enough to get maximum enjoyment of the smell and the lights. Our past Christmas trees always brought a sense of happiness, memories of family and friends, and lots of joy. Even though it had only been a month and a half since his death, I wanted to continue our traditions. I wanted a tree. Continuing our traditions helped me believe that my life didn't end with his.

The day after Thanksgiving came, and I woke up anxious to get a tree. I was confident that it would make me feel better. I was tired of carrying this endless sadness on my shoulders. I wanted to remember the previous years when I brought a tree home. My loved one would give his approval before later complaining that the tree was too big for the space.

I dressed for the mild 55-degree temperature and took the

259

one-mile drive to the local Christmas tree farm. Upon arrival, I walked through the farm, scanning the trees as I had done in the past. I quickly realized that I was no longer enthusiastic about this venture. All I wanted to do was get a tree – any tree. I picked the closest one to me, and the attendant cut it and tied it to my car.

Upon arrival home, I found that everything about this adventure was exhausting. I removed the tree from my car, walked inside, and moved the furniture around to accommodate it. Summoning the energy, I dragged the tree into the house. It took multiple tries to get the tree straight in the stand, and once I was finished, I began to cry. Nothing about this search for the beautiful tree felt the same. Whatever illusion I had at the beginning of the day no longer existed. All I knew was that I was alone, I would be decorating this tree alone, and I wouldn't be hearing my loved one's voice complaining about the size of this tree. I had to remind myself that yes, I was alone, and yes, I would be decorating this tree alone, but I had no idea how I would feel once it was trimmed and beautiful.

I sat down and just looked at the tree. It wasn't the most beautiful tree I had ever bought with its empty spaces, saggy limbs, not symmetrical or as tall as our trees in the past. However, what it did give me was the hope that tomorrow I'd have the energy to put on the twinkle lights. Maybe by just acting "as if" all would be okay, and I would one day enjoy this tradition – my tradition – again.

126

So This is Christmas

*"We don't really have any big family traditions; just spending
time with each other is the most important part."*
~ Madison Beer

It was Christmas Eve, and I found myself at the dining room
table, overlooking the woods around my home. The house was decorated for the holidays, the fireplace was lit, and that warm glow of
soft white twinkle lights could be seen throughout the downstairs.
If I focused only on this moment, it was beautiful.

As a child, I longed for the Christmas celebrations that my
classmates would speak of because mine were never like that.
Growing up in a Latin household, Christmas was celebrated on
Christmas Eve. We got together with other family members to
feast on traditional foods and occasionally dance. Gifts were exchanged that night. Despite the unique celebration, I wanted the
Christmas celebration my classmates described.

Through the years, I slowly incorporated the things I wanted
to see or experience into my Christmas holiday. But the significant changes took place after the birth of my son, and, like parents
everywhere, I tried to make his Christmas as memorable as I could.
There was something magical about the anticipation on his face as

261

he patiently waited to open a gift. When I married, experiencing Christmas through my husband's eyes was initially a challenge; however, as the years passed, I saw that magical look on his face too.

It's probably no surprise that I wanted a fantastic first big holiday with this new blended family. I wanted my loved one to be as excited as I was to decorate the tree, put up as many twinkle lights as our home could hold, and have our family seated around the dining room table. It never occurred to me that he truly despised the holidays.

So we talked about it, and he shared his experience. For the first time, I saw the holiday through the eyes of a frightened child facing a Christmas season full of marital discord, infidelity, and lots of drinking. I knew I couldn't change what he had experienced in the past, but I asked that he keep an open mind and participate. He agreed.

In the years before his death, the holiday spirit was made tangible by the beautiful trees, abundant twinkle lights, and the warm glow of our fireplace. The joy that accompanied this mental picture was palpable, overwhelming, and truly magical. Regardless of what we did, we both knew the real joy was being surrounded by our family.

But our children to have families of their own and their lives took them to various parts of the States. We were no longer physically close to each other. My beloved and I had very small and intimate celebration, but continued our traditions on a smaller scale: wearing the Santa hats, one gift on the eve, and the remainder on Christmas day. I would make a special breakfast and we would sit to enjoy the food and our wonderful view of the woods. We would have a gentle snowfall to watch if we were really lucky.

This year the realization of a different picture set in: that my son and his wife had traveled to Italy and would be spending Christmas in Rome and my daughter would spend it with her husband and beautiful daughters at their California home. This year would be different, and I was not looking forward to waking up to a house filled with sorrow and loneliness.

I glanced to the end of my dining room table and saw The Hat. Unsure what to do with it, I had taken the Santa hat out of the ornament box a month before and laid it on the table. This hat had a history in our family. I'm not going to say he enjoyed wearing it, but he looked forward to seeing me happy as he wore it.

But now I find myself sitting alone in front of the fire, putting on his Santa hat, reminiscing about past happy holidays, and knowing that era is gone forever. My loved one would never again wear this hat, nor would he be handing out the presents this Christmas Eve. Mercifully, as negativity started to rise, my thoughts changed.

I felt the corners of my mouth form a smile as I thought about what the wearing of that Santa Hat had done for my family. Our families embraced this tiny holiday tradition. As insignificant and trivial as it seemed, the tradition has moved on and thrives in our daughter's and son's families Thinking of how much joy it actually brought – and continues to bring – makes me smile even more. I'm genuinely grateful for our little family tradition and thankful that it didn't die with my loved one.

The next morning I awoke to a beautiful blue sky and a light dusting of snow. As soon as I opened my eyes, I said a quick prayer. I started a fire, turned on the twinkle lights, and immediately the glow and warmth filled both my heart and my home. There were no presents to unwrap, and I did not put on my Santa hat but both my breakfast and the view were picture perfect. I knew a generous god had blessed me with gifts this morning: a brief reprieve from sorrow and a beautiful white Christmas.

127

From Gratitude to Grace

I sometimes struggle to find just the right words to accurately express the feelings I so vividly remember. I've been able to share some of my experiences, hoping to convey that there's hope. Even in the deepest sadness, there lies a simple promise: another day, another attitude, or another feeling is always available. Sometimes we need help to find them. Sometimes we need tools.

I have found that the power of affirmation has helped me get to the other side of my grief and replace negative thoughts with some hope.

To help me cope with my loss, I created little signs around my house. They were short phrases to remind me that not only would I survive, but eventually, I would also thrive. Venturing into the kitchen for a drink of water or the bathroom to comb my hair, I'd see a phrase offering the courage, faith, and resilience to meet the next difficult moment. As strange as it may seem, I would make myself read it aloud. There was something about hearing myself repeat positive, optimistic thoughts that eventually enabled me to heal and experience hope.

I offer the following pages with the hope that you find an affirmation – or several – that work for you. Speak or write them as if the thoughts or behaviors they represent already exist in your life.

265

Initially, you may not feel anything positive, and that's absolutely fine. I began utilizing them even though I did not immediately feel the hope I craved. With time and practice, it came.

As you grow in peace with a situation, a thought, or an emotion, remember to choose a new affirmation or two. I imagine that there will come a time when you create affirmations of your own. Remember, they should always be personal, positive, and present tense.

I'd love it if you send it my way – I'm picturing a page on my website with a large list of community-created affirmations to wrap around those who will come later.

Affirmations

I pray for continued courage to walk through these first few days.

I am making calls from my to-do list and trust this will get me through another day.

I embrace my feelings and understand that I have been blessed with emotions for the privilege of living. Today I am feeling them.

I walk through another day with the determination to adjust to my new life.

I embrace the courage that has gotten me through this first night alone.

I give myself permission to let go of as many things as I need to without judgment.

I am grateful for the people who have been kind, tolerant, and compassionate during this challenging time.

I embrace the joy of preparing a special meal, and I am grateful for the few hours of reprieve from my grief.

I survive all the firsts – birthdays, anniversaries, holidays, and the like.

I am grateful for every day I am alive.

I meditate to get in touch with the peaceful moments in my life.

I am patient and have faith that my life will get better.

I embrace the support that others provide and thank them for their selflessness.

I continue to accept the feelings about my loss without judgment, knowing that this too shall pass.

I am vulnerable and truthful in my support group, believing it will provide hope to others experiencing loss.

I believe in my journey and trust that happiness will be part of my future.

I express my profound appreciation to my family and friends for being there for my loved one and myself.

I visit my loved one's grave, leaving a little of my grief behind.

I am grateful to accomplish his last request knowing he trusted me to get it done.

I am grateful for the mortal blessings that walked into our home and lives.

I am blessed to have been present for the last breath.

I will handle whatever is ahead.

I will feel it in my heart when the time comes to remove my wedding ring.

I am grateful for the courage to feel his love and let a little of my grief go.

I am indebted to those who extended invitations and made me feel a part of their families.

I am grateful for the last moments with my loved one.

I am thankful for the people in my path who supported and loved me through the first year.

I am healing, and when it is right, I will enjoy an evening out. I am comforted that others can enjoy the tickets that I could not.

I am grateful that our traditions are bring joy to my loved ones.

I commit to leaving uncomfortable memories at the door and entering my new life with love.

I am indebted to my friends and will let them know at every opportunity.

I am grateful for the kindness and compassion afforded me by others.

I let go of my expectations of others.

I am thankful that at this present moment, I feel happy.

I am grateful for the gift of peace and tranquility on this day.

I hold onto the small things that carry me through another day of healing.

I get through this first New Year's Day focusing on my inner strength.

I am courageous to participate in things that make me unsure.

I am thankful for my evening out with a friend and the memories of love that surfaced today.

I focus on feelings of love and choose gratitude over sadness.

I breathe in the healing love of my memories.

I am of service to others.

I am blessed for the friends who love me unconditionally and support me through my grief process.

I embrace every moment of reprieve from the pain.

I am grateful for the lightheartedness provided by the concert I attended.

I focus on hope and pray for courage to keep moving forward in my grief process.

I commit to feeling my feelings without judgment and remembering one thought of happiness that warms my heart.

I focus on the memories of the good that happened.

I welcome the experience of others and how they coped with the loss of a spouse.

I believe I will smile, laugh and enjoy my life again.

I pray for the courage and humility to ask for help.

I ask for help when I'm confused about my feelings.

I pray for peace and recognition of the blessings in my life.

I am grieving but will not forget the love we shared.

I am patient and wait for my perspective to change.

I am grateful for the awareness that today has brought.

I reach out to my support system when I find myself wanting to run away.

I am grateful for the temporary gift of the life we shared.

I embrace the person I am today.

I accept the wisdom that defining moments bring to my life.

I give myself permission to be where I am.

I am grateful for the supervisor who cared enough to pick up the phone and speak to HR on my behalf.

I nurture my relationships.

I see the gifts in my life.

I am grateful for a loving and trusting relationship with my long-time friend.

I look for the best in people.

I am privileged to have a wonderful group of women in my life and beyond grateful for the unconditional love shown me through my grief.

I am grateful for my blessings on this day.

I show my gratitude to my coworkers by being there for them as they were there for me.

I share my truth and allow my friends to support me during this difficult time.

I embrace the love shared on Facebook posts regarding the loss of my loved one.

I am grateful for the kindness of my friend and for having fulfilled my unspoken promise to my loved one.

I search for the right words in difficult situations and embrace every moment of love I share with my children.

I am grateful to see the positive in my life.

I reach out to friends when I start feeling broken or damaged.

I thank the god of my understanding for my mentor and her wisdom.

I am grateful for the privilege of being a mentor to some wonderful women.

I am thankful for opportunities to show up for my friends.

I am grateful to see how willingness is works in my life.

I am grateful for my unintended path and the memories that led me here.

I recreate the joy that dinner parties brought to my life and commit to start entertaining again.

I focus on the calm, peace, and intimacy my home provides.

I am grateful for the memories of love for my loved one.

I embrace the uncertainty of my current life, trusting that all will work out the way it is supposed to.

I am grateful for the trips made with my loved one.

I commit to visiting new museums and galleries.

I show my gratitude by living every moment to its fullest.

I am grateful for the passion my loved one had for his painting and the scent of oil paints that permeated our lives.

I thank my god for the love that surrounded me on this day.

I am grateful for my personal storybook ending and the detours that got me here.

I am grateful for the silly memories.

271

I embrace the unwavering support of friends.

I focus on the blessings that my losses brought to my life, knowing the amount of pain has been proportional to the amount of love we shared.

I am grateful for memories of my loved one that music conjures up.

I let go of the insignificant things that keep me in pain.

I am blessed to have loved an artist.

I am grateful for the multicolored fingerprints he left on my heart.

I complete the essential tasks ahead of me despite my uneasiness.

I reach out for assistance when overwhelmed.

I am patient as I wait for a time when I can again enjoy a meal with or without company.

I seek opportunities for self-care with the same compassion that I showed my loved one.

I pray for wisdom to make appropriate choices regarding my loved one's possessions.

I seek guidance from others when I am unsure.

I take the necessary actions for my well-being.

I meditate to identify my limitations and for the courage to walk through them.

I embrace my new life.

I take the care to lovingly prepare my next meal.

I thank my god for putting people in my life who have my best interest at heart.

I walk through my discomfort, knowing this will pass.

I walk in faith, releasing my grief to the god of my understanding.

I adjust to my new life and accept that, for today, I am a 'Table for One.'

I focus on the tasks at hand and my willingness to be productive.

I am grateful that no decision needs to be rushed or made today.

I feel my grief and hope that I will one day awaken without this heaviness in my heart.

I embrace this wonderful peaceful day.

I grab the hope that prayer and meditation bring.

I accept and recognize that these tears are a blessing, are healing, and make me human.

I am grateful for the opportunity to be the caretaker of my loved one's writing.

I focus on things that keep me grateful.

I walk through difficult mornings with courage and determination.

I thank God for the opportunities to see the benefits of acceptance.

I stay in the present and do not run from what I feel.

I pray for peace and celebrate the happiness of others.

I am grateful for the honesty and our joint decisions which brought us closer together.

I do no harm despite how I feel.

I am grateful that my passion returned to my work life.

I nurture the beginnings of passion as they appear in all areas of my life.

I embrace not knowing what comes next and trust I am fine.

I pray for healing and not judge seeking professional help for my grief.

I search for pictures that make me smile and provide memories of a life well-lived.

I let go of the guilt and shame for things not said.

I practice self-care by focusing on being still.

I accept that changes happen as I am ready.

I welcome people back into my home and my life.

I nurture myself with love ensuring my emotional, spiritual, and physical selves are attended to.

I am grateful for the courage and the determination to walk through the things that make me uncomfortable.

I am indebted for memories of my loved one, which made me smile.

I am grateful for this moment when peace entered my heart.

I am thankful that I have long-term friends who love me no matter what.

I am grateful for the glimpse that showed me love is still part of my life.

I am responsible for the direction that my life is headed.

I embrace my evening out, my friend, and the ability to leave my broken heart at the door.

I am comforted by the peace meditation brought to this moment.

I continue to practice compassion towards myself.

I embrace the courage of my past as it got me through his illnesses and subsequent death.

I enjoy all moments of happiness that come into my life.

I meet my new life with courage.

I accept vulnerability and pray for the courage to share how I really feel.

I believe in the peace the garden provides.

I am grateful for the ability to reach out to friends.

I commit to the temporary discomfort of therapy, believing the work will allow me to move on with my life.

I am grateful for the closeness our family hugs brought.

I focus on the kindness in my heart.

I am thankful that my loved one's suffering is over.

I focus on the healing of my soul.

I am blessed by a glimpse into the beauty of my new life.

I embrace the courage to find my happiness and live my life in the present.

Thank you for reading!

Rosina Leigh Eller and Dodge Pond Press hope you have enjoyed this book, and if you are grieving may it bring you hope and comfort.

If you like what you've read, please consider posting your comments on the social media sites of your choice, and on your favorite booksellers' websites.

For more information about the author, or to offer
your comments directly, please visit her website:

https://rosinaleigheller.com

Made in the USA
Las Vegas, NV
11 June 2022

50094993R00164